Christian W. Martin

Visual data mining in intrinsic hierarchical complex biodata

Christian W. Martin

Visual data mining in intrinsic hierarchical complex biodata

Novel approaches for analyzing gene expression data in biomedicine and sequence data in metagenomics

Südwestdeutscher Verlag für Hochschulschriften

Impressum/Imprint (nur für Deutschland/ only for Germany)
Bibliografische Information der Deutschen Nationalbibliothek: Die Deutsche Nationalbibliothek verzeichnet diese Publikation in der Deutschen Nationalbibliografie; detaillierte bibliografische Daten sind im Internet über http://dnb.d-nb.de abrufbar.
Alle in diesem Buch genannten Marken und Produktnamen unterliegen warenzeichen-, marken- oder patentrechtlichem Schutz bzw. sind Warenzeichen oder eingetragene Warenzeichen der jeweiligen Inhaber. Die Wiedergabe von Marken, Produktnamen, Gebrauchsnamen, Handelsnamen, Warenbezeichnungen u.s.w. in diesem Werk berechtigt auch ohne besondere Kennzeichnung nicht zu der Annahme, dass solche Namen im Sinne der Warenzeichen- und Markenschutzgesetzgebung als frei zu betrachten wären und daher von jedermann benutzt werden dürften.

Verlag: Südwestdeutscher Verlag für Hochschulschriften Aktiengesellschaft & Co. KG
Dudweiler Landstr. 99, 66123 Saarbrücken, Deutschland
Telefon +49 681 37 20 271-1, Telefax +49 681 37 20 271-0, Email: info@svh-verlag.de
Zugl.: Bielefeld, Universität, Diss., 2009

Herstellung in Deutschland:
Schaltungsdienst Lange o.H.G., Zehrensdorfer Str. 11, D-12277 Berlin
Books on Demand GmbH, Gutenbergring 53, D-22848 Norderstedt
Reha GmbH, Dudweiler Landstr. 99, D- 66123 Saarbrücken
ISBN: 978-3-8381-0979-4

Imprint (only for USA, GB)
Bibliographic information published by the Deutsche Nationalbibliothek: The Deutsche Nationalbibliothek lists this publication in the Deutsche Nationalbibliografie; detailed bibliographic data are available in the Internet at http://dnb.d-nb.de.
Any brand names and product names mentioned in this book are subject to trademark, brand or patent protection and are trademarks or registered trademarks of their respective holders. The use of brand names, product names, common names, trade names, product descriptions etc. even without
a particular marking in this works is in no way to be construed to mean that such names may be regarded as unrestricted in respect of trademark and brand protection legislation and could thus be used by anyone.

Publisher:
Südwestdeutscher Verlag für Hochschulschriften Aktiengesellschaft & Co. KG
Dudweiler Landstr. 99, 66123 Saarbrücken, Germany
Phone +49 681 37 20 271-1, Fax +49 681 37 20 271-0, Email: info@svh-verlag.de

Copyright © 2008 Südwestdeutscher Verlag für Hochschulschriften Aktiengesellschaft & Co. KG and licensors
All rights reserved. Saarbrücken 2008

Produced in USA and UK by:
Lightning Source Inc., 1246 Heil Quaker Blvd., La Vergne, TN 37086, USA
Lightning Source UK Ltd., Chapter House, Pitfield, Kiln Farm, Milton Keynes, MK11 3LW, GB
BookSurge, 7290 B. Investment Drive, North Charleston, SC 29418, USA
ISBN: 978-3-8381-0979-4

This thesis is dedicated to my wife Mireille, to my mother Monika and my father Wolfgang, to my sisters Alexandra and Eva, and to the memories of my grandfathers Hugo and Johannes.

Acknowledgement

At this point, I would like to thank those people that supported me during my PhD thesis. First of all, my special thanks appertain to my supervisors Junior-Prof. Tim Wilhelm Nattkemper and Prof. Anke Becker for their constant support, valuable input and fruitful discussions at different stages of this work.
Furthermore, I am highly grateful to Naryttza N. Diaz and Anika Tauchen for the close and productive collaboration and for introducing me to the interesting world of modern genetics and metagenomics. I would also like to thank Harmen grosse Deters for his important contribution in terms of his diploma thesis as well as Joerg Ontrup for his fast H^2SOM training algorithm and visualization framework.
My thanks also appertain to the International Graduate School for Bioinformatics and Genome Research of the University of Bielefeld and the federal state North Rhine-Westphalia for financial support and the abundance of interesting talks and seminars. The data processed in this work was provided by the US National Center for Biotechnology Information (NCBI), Rosetta Inpharmatics, the Broad Institute, and in collaboration with the Städtische Kliniken Bielefeld. I would also like to thank Wiebke Timm, Anika Tauchen, Naryttza N. Diaz, Tim W. Nattkemper, Andre Martin and Mireille Martin for proofreading parts of the manuscript. Thanks also to all members of the Applied Neuroinformatics Group and the Graduate School for the inspiriting and enjoyable working place.
On the personal side, my deepest gratefulness holds for my wife Mireille Martin for all her support and encouragement as well as for my son Laurin, who granted me some time slots once in a while that allowed me to finish writing this thesis. Finally, I would also like to thank my parents, my sisters as well as all my friends for their support and the interesting and manifold discussions.

Summary

In the present work, novel visual data mining approaches for the analysis of intrinsic hierarchical complex biodata are developed. Application of these methods is presented for gene expression data in biomedicine as well as for sequence data in metagenomics.

Complex biological data is characterized by a high dimensionality, multimodality, missing values and noisiness, making its analysis a challenging task. It consists of *primary data*, the core data produced by a modern high-throughput technology, and *secondary data*, a collection of all kinds of respective supplementary data and background knowledge. Furthermore, biological data often has an intrinsic hierarchical structure (e.g. species in the Tree of Life), an important property that should be considered when developing novel approaches for complex data analysis.

Machine learning offers a wide range of computer algorithms to extract structural patterns from existing complex data to address the issues the biomedical researcher is interested in. Algorithms are adapted and developed such that both primary and secondary data are taken into account while at the same time insights into the analyzed data can be obtained. To this end, indices for cluster validation as well as methods for visualization enhancement are developed.

In this work, a *Tree Index (TI)* is developed for the external validation of hierarchical clustering results to support the analysis of gene expression data. The TI is extended to the Normalized Tree Index (NTI) to identify correlations between clustered primary data and external labels. Also, the REEFSOM (Nattkemper, 2005) is adapted to integrate clustered gene expression data, clinical data and categorical data in one display.

In the domain of sequence analysis and metagenomics, a Self-Organizing Map (SOM) classifier is developed in hyperbolic space to classify small variable-length DNA fragments. For this task, 350 prokaryotic organisms at six taxonomic levels in the Tree of Life are used. Finally, studies about the capabilities of SOMs to reassess the structural organization of the prokaryotic organisms in the Tree of Life are performed in both Euclidean and hyperbolic space.

Zusammenfassung

In der vorliegenden Arbeit werden neue Ansätze des visuellen Dataminings zur Analyse von intrinsisch hierarchischen komplexen Biodaten entwickelt. Die Anwendung dieser Verfahren wird anhand von Genexpressionsdaten aus dem Bereich der Biomedizin sowie von Gensequenzdaten im Bereich der Metagenomik gezeigt.

Komplexe biologische Daten sind charakterisiert durch eine hohe Dimensionalität, Multimodalität, fehlende Werte und Rauschen, wodurch die Analyse dieser Daten deutlich erschwert wird. Sie lassen sich in *Primärdaten* (Kerndaten bzw. Messwerte, die durch moderne Technologien in hoher Zahl erzeugt werden) und *Sekundärdaten* (ergänzende Daten, Zusatzinformationen und Hintergrundwissen) unterteilen. Zudem weisen biologische Daten oftmals eine innere hierarchische Struktur auf (z.B. Spezies im Baum des Lebens). Diese Eigenschaft sollte bei der Entwicklung neuer Ansätze zur Analyse komplexer Daten berücksichtigt werden.

Im Bereich des maschinellen Lernens steht eine grosse Zahl von Computeralgorithmen zur Verfügung, um diejenigen strukturelle Muster aus existierenden komplexen Daten zu extrahieren, an denen der Forscher interessiert ist. In dieser Arbeit werden bestehende Algorithmen angepasst sowie neue entwickelt, die sowohl Primär- als auch Sekundärdaten in die Auswertung einbeziehen und gleichzeitig Einsicht in die analysierten Daten gewähren. Dazu werden Gütemasse zur Clustervalidierung sowie Visualisierungstechniken entwickelt.

In dieser Arbeit wird der *Tree Index (TI)* für die externe Validierung hierarchisch geclusterter Daten entwickelt, um die Analyse von Genexpressionsdaten zu unterstützen. Der TI wird zum Normalisierten Tree Index erweitert (NTI) mit dessen Hilfe sich Korrelationen zwischen geclusterten Primärdaten und externen Labels identifizieren lassen. Anwendung findet ausserdem die sog. REEFSOM (Nattkemper, 2005), welche adaptiert wird, um geclusterte Gendaten, klinische Daten und kategorische Daten in einer Darstellung zu integrieren.

Auf dem Gebiet der Gensequenzanalyse wird ein Klassifikator für die Selbst-Organisierende Karte (SOM) im hyperbolischen Raum entwickelt, mit dem kleine DNA-Fragmente variabler Länge klassifiziert werden können. Hierfür werden 350 prokaryotische Organismen auf sechs taxonomischen Ebenen im Baum des Lebens verwendet. Zum Schluss wird gezeigt, inwieweit SOMs im euklidischen und im hyperbolischen Raum in der Lage sind, die strukturelle Organisation der prokaryotischen Organismen im Baum des Lebens abzubilden.

Publications

Parts of this thesis have been published in advance in:

- **Martin, C.**, Diaz, N. N., Ontrup, J., and Nattkemper, T. W. (2008). *Hyperbolic SOM-based clustering of DNA fragment features for taxonomic visualization and classification.* Bioinformatics, Vol. 24, 1568 - 1574.

- **Martin, C.**, and Nattkemper, T. W. (2008). *A Tree Index to Support Clustering Based Exploratory Data Analysis.* 2nd Intern. Conf. on Bioinformatics Research and Development (BIRD).

- **Martin, C.**, Diaz, N. N., Ontrup, J., and Nattkemper, T. W. (2007). *Genome feature exploration using hyperbolic Self-Organizing Maps.* WSOM.

- **Martin, C.**, grosse Deters, H., and Nattkemper, T. W. (2006). *Fusing biomedical multi-modal data for exploratory data analysis.* ICANN, Part II, LNCS 4132, 798-807.

- **Martin, C.**, grosse Deters, H., and Nattkemper, T. W. (2006). *Exploratory analysis of multi-modal data including breast cancer microarray data.* ISMB (Poster)

It should be noted that the first and the third publication as well as the work of chapters 8 and 9 is based on preparatory and pioneering work of Naryttza N. Diaz[1].

Software

- An implementation of the Tree Index in Matlab as proposed in chapter 5 can be downloaded at:

  www.techfak.uni-bielefeld.de/ags/ani/projects/TreeIndex/

- An implementation of the H^{2}SOM classifier in Matlab as proposed in chapter 8 is provided at:

  www.techfak.uni-bielefeld.de/ags/ani/projects/HHSOMSeqData/

---

[1]Center for Biotechnology, University of Bielefeld

Contents

1	**Introduction**	**1**
1.1	Chapter overview	6
2	**Machine learning algorithms**	**8**
2.1	Hierarchical Agglomerative Clustering	9
2.2	Spectral Clustering	10
	2.2.1 Normalized cuts	10
	2.2.2 Future Perspectives of spectral clustering	13
2.3	Self-Organizing Maps	14
	2.3.1 SOM types	16
	2.3.2 SOM classifier	18
2.4	Topology Preservation for SOMs	20
	2.4.1 Topographic error	20
	2.4.2 Quantification error and distortion	21
	2.4.3 Trustworthiness and Discontinuities	21
	2.4.4 Measures based on correlations of distances	23
2.5	k-nearest neighbor classifier	23
3	**Data**	**25**
3.1	DNA Microarray technology	25
	3.1.1 Intensity-dependent normalization	26
	3.1.2 Visualization	27
3.2	Sequence and taxonomic data	27
	3.2.1 DNA sequence data	28
	3.2.2 Sanger sequencing	29
	3.2.3 454 Pyrosequencing	29
	3.2.4 Nanopores	30
	3.2.5 Genetic material used in this thesis	30
	3.2.6 Taxonomy	31
4	**Cluster Validation**	**38**
4.1	Internal cluster indices	39
	4.1.1 intra- and inter-cluster variance	40

		4.1.2	Calinski Harabasz Index	41
		4.1.3	Index I	42
		4.1.4	Separation	43
		4.1.5	Silhouette Width	43
		4.1.6	Davis-Bouldin index	44
		4.1.7	Dunn's index	44
		4.1.8	C Index	45
		4.1.9	Goodman-Kruskal Index	45
	4.2	External cluster indices		45
	4.3	Cluster validation bias		49
	4.4	Stability of clustering results		49

5 The Tree Index   51

- 5.1 Methods … 52
- 5.2 Results … 57
  - 5.2.1 Simulated data … 57
  - 5.2.2 Real-world Cancer data sets … 58
- 5.3 Theoretical considerations … 63
  - 5.3.1 Tree structures and leaf orderings … 63
  - 5.3.2 Different scoring methodologies … 66
  - 5.3.3 The probability of a split … 66
  - 5.3.4 Cumulative hypergeometric distribution … 67
- 5.4 Discussion … 68
  - 5.4.1 Outlook … 68

6 Normalized Tree Index   72

- 6.1 Methods … 75
  - 6.1.1 The Normalized Tree Index (NTI) … 75
  - 6.1.2 p-value … 75
- 6.2 Results … 78
- 6.3 Discussion … 81

7 Fusing biomedical multi-modal data   89

- 7.1 SOM-based sea bed rendering … 90
- 7.2 The fish glyph … 91
- 7.3 Application … 94
  - 7.3.1 Mapping … 95
  - 7.3.2 Results … 95
- 7.4 Summary and Discussion … 96

8 Taxonomic classification of DNA fragments   99

- 8.1 Feature vector computation … 102
  - 8.1.1 Normalization … 104
- 8.2 Results … 106

	8.3 Feature selection	113
	8.4 Discussion	115
9	**Reassessing the tree of life**	**118**
	9.1 Material and methods	119
	9.2 Results	120
	9.3 Summary and discussion	124
10	**Conclusion**	**125**
	10.1 Future prospects	126

Chapter 1

Introduction

Science in the 21st century is characterized by huge amounts of data obtained by novel technologies in almost full automation. Exponential decreasing prices for storage capacities allow the collection of all types of measured data. At the same time, data from different experiments obtained at different places can easily be linked thanks to computer networking. By analyzing the resulting large collections of data sets, many new insights in various domains are expected. One field that is characterized by revolutionary progress in recent years is the field of molecular biology. Novel high-throughput technologies for sequencing and the measuring of gene expressions inter alia allow the automated generation of large data collections at exponentially decreasing periods and prices. Many new insights into life are expected from an evaluation of these large data collections. However, especially in biomedicine, a decent analysis of such data is a challenging task.

Biomedical data is often characterized by a highly complex structure: First, it has a high amount of noise due to natural variations as they are omnipresent in nature. Second, it is high-dimensional because of the large amounts of data produced by novel technologies. The high dimensionality is even amplified by ultra-fast developments of several technologies leading to an exponential increase of data. Third, missing values are omnipresent due to incomplete biological samples. Finally, it is multi-modal because data sets from different sources and of different structures and sizes are combined with background knowledge from the specific field of research. In order to analyze this highly complex biomedical data in a thorough way, novel algorithmic approaches are required.

Complex biomedical data can be categorized into *primary data* and *secondary data*. Primary data is obtained in the main experiment by a novel high-throughput technology. The two most common types of primary data are *measurement data* and *sequence data*. Measurement data consists of up to millions of measurements obtained in one or multiple experiments and

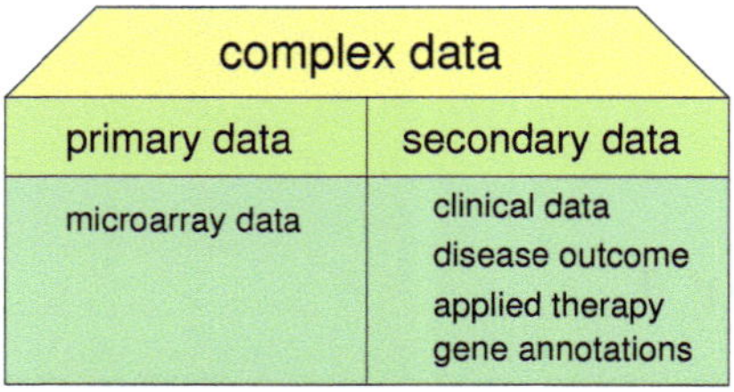

Figure 1.1: Complex biomedical data can be categorized into *primary data* and *secondary data*. The primary data is obtained in the main experiment whereas the secondary data includes all supplementary data about the analyzed subjects. In this example the primary data is gene expression data from microarray experiments. The corresponding secondary data consists of clinical data, disease outcome, informations about the applied therapy, as well as gene annotations.

can be summarized in a vector or a matrix. Sequence data is stored as a string over an alphabet, e.g. a DNA sequence is described by a string over nucleotides and a protein is described by a string over the amino acids. All available supplementary data about the subject matter of interest supporting the analysis of the primary data is denoted as secondary data in this thesis. Secondary data is a heterogeneous collection of all kinds of data items, data sets, annotation data about the analyzed subjects as well as background knowledge from various sources. Thus, secondary data usually has a different structure than the primary data (Figure 1.1).

Major challenges arise from the availability of complex biomedical data collections: How can the researcher analyze the primary data in combination with the available secondary data consisting of different data types, sizes and dimensions? How can the noisy multi-modal high-dimensional biomedical data be analyzed in an integrative manner to discover unknown structures and patterns?

In the presented thesis, novel approaches for the data-driven analysis of complex data are developed. Example applications are presented on complex biomedical data of two major fields in current genetics and metagenomics: analysis of gene expression data and sequence analysis. In the first field, primary data is obtained by DNA microarray technology. By measuring the activity of tens of thousands of genes for hundreds of subjects in multiple experiments, high-dimensional measurement data is produced. The corresponding secondary data is composed of additional information about the analyzed subjects and genes. This is clinical data, disease outcome for each subject as well as gene annotation data for each gene.

In sequence analysis, primary data consists of sequence data obtained from novel high-throughput sequencing technologies, i.e. Sanger sequencing (Sanger et al., 1977) and 454 Pyrosequencing (Margulies et al., 2005). The resulting assembled DNA sequences contain up to several millions of base pairs for every sequenced species. The corresponding secondary data encloses knowledge about the respective phenotypes, e.g. taxonomic information for most organisms is offered by phylogenetics.

In general, data analysis can be approached in three different ways: manually, automatically and interactively. A manual evaluation of complex data is usually infeasible because of the high dimensionality of the data. Even though complex data can be stored in tables and databases, only a fraction of hidden patterns can be revealed this way. An automatic analysis is only applicable to a limited extend due to the heterogeneous structure and the multi-modality of the complex biomedical data. Also, background knowledge cannot be incorporated in an automated analysis process. In contrast to that, the interactive approach enables to include background knowledge of the biomedical researcher while allowing the application of various evaluation methods at the same time.

Machine learning, which is a subfield of artificial intelligence, combines methods from data mining, pattern recognition, neuroinformatics, and statistics (Duda et al., 2001; Hastie et al., 2001; Bishop, 2007). A wide range of computer algorithms has been developed to extract structural patterns from existing complex data to address the issues the biomedical researcher is interested in. Machine learning algorithms can be grouped into methods for supervised learning, i.e. classification, and those for unsupervised learning, i.e. clustering.

In supervised learning, a classifier builds an internal model based on labeled training data, which subsequently allows to classify new unlabeled data. In terms of complex data, the primary data can be used as training data whereas the respective labels are provided by a selected modality of the secondary data. The intention of a classifier is to achieve the highest rate of correct classifications. A drawback of supervised learning is that the classification rate does not reveal any information about the internal structure of the data and thus does not allow a further inspection. In unsupervised learning, cluster algorithms are applied to detect natural groups and structure in the primary data, without making use of the secondary data. Cluster algorithms are useful tools to uncover hidden structures and patterns in the primary data. The knowledge gained this way can be used to obtain a better understanding of the data and can help to improve classification results when applied prior to classification.

The different scopes of supervised and unsupervised learning confront the bio-medical researcher with the following difficulty: Supervised learning takes both primary and secondary data into account without providing any further insights into the internal structure of the data. Unsupervised learning only takes the primary data into account without using the secondary data.

In the presented thesis, machine learning algorithms are developed that take both primary and secondary data into account while at the same time providing insights into the analyzed data. The primary objective is to uncover hidden structures and patterns in the complex data by taking all available data about the subject matter of interest into consideration. The maximization of classification rates is a successive task and is of minor importance in this thesis. In two different approaches, secondary data is combined with clustered primary data: cluster validation and visualization enhancement [1].

Cluster algorithms detect structure in any data, even if there is none. Cluster validation allows to compensate this major weakness of cluster algorithms. Cluster validation indices can be grouped into *internal* and *external cluster indices*. Internal cluster indices validate clustering results by making use of the same data that has been used for clustering. External cluster indices use external information to compute the quality of the clustering result and thus allow a more objective validation of the clustering result. The availability of secondary data provides the chance to use it for an external validation.

Most cluster algorithms provide some sort of visualization of their results. This visualization feasibility to visually inspect the clustered data is probably one of the most important motivations for the usage of cluster algorithms. Thus, a second major approach to combine secondary data with clustered primary data is to enhance the clustering result visualization. The application of hierarchical agglomerative clustering to display gene expression data (Eisen et al., 1998) is one favorite example for enhancing the visualization of clustered primary data through secondary data. In the visualization of the clustered gene expression data (primary data), the tree branches are colored according to gene functions (secondary data).

When choosing machine learning algorithms for the analysis of complex data, the potential underlying data structures of the primary data are of major importance. In biomedicine, a predominant and likely intrinsic structure is the hierarchical organization of entities. The most prominent example for such a hierarchical organization is probably the Tree of Life in which all species are organized in a tree-like structure. The major categorization of species is captured on the first level whereas finer differentiations are obtained at lower levels. Human tissue can also be structured in a hierarchical way: On the first level, it can be divided into normal and tumor tissue. On the second level, tumor tissue can be grouped into different tumor types or in benign and malignant tumors. Malignant tumors can further be categorized as tumors that produce metastasis and those that do not. Depending

---

[1]This approach should not be confused with semi-supervised learning, which aims to improve the classification error of a classifier by adding large amounts of unlabeled data to the labeled data set.

on the domain, more specific categorizations exist, i.e. breast cancer tumors can be divided into lubular and ductal tumors or into tumors with positive and negative lymph nodes. Even though a hierarchical organization has often been observed in complex biomedical data, this property cannot be assumed but has to be proven. Machine learning algorithms play a crucial role in detecting certain intrinsic structures such as hierarchy in the data.
In the presented thesis, novel approaches for visual data mining for the analysis of intrinsic hierarchical complex biodata are developed. Thereby, the following issues are discussed:

- How can primary and secondary data be taken into account while at the same time providing insights into the analyzed data?
- How can machine learning algorithms be applied to integrate noisy, high-dimensional and multi-modal primary and secondary data in order to gain new insights into life?
- How can hidden structures and patterns be uncovered in complex data?
- How can hierarchical structure be detected?

In the first area of application, the field of gene expression data analysis, investigations on the following issues are made:

- Can hierarchical clustered primary data be validated using secondary data?
- Is it possible to detect correlations between primary and secondary data, despite their diverse structure and high dimensionality?
- Can both primary and secondary data be visualized in one display to allow a further inspection of the complex data?

In the second area of application, the field of sequence analysis and metagenomics, the following issues are addressed:

- Can a hierarchical structure be observed in sequence data?
- Can this information be used to classify short sequence reads on different taxonomic levels?

1.1 Chapter overview

In Chapter 2, the machine learning algorithms that are used throughout this thesis are summarized. Unsupervised learning methods (hierarchical agglomerative clustering, spectral clustering, Self-Organizing Maps (SOM) in Euclidean and hyperbolic space), supervised learning methods (SOM classifier and k-nearest neighbor classifier) as well as methods to compute the topology preservation of trained SOMs are presented.

Chapter 3 describes the data used in this thesis and the technologies that have been used for its generation. The DNA microarray technology that allows to simultaneously measure the expressions of tens of thousands of genes in tissue samples is introduced in section 3.1. A short overview about modern high-throughput sequencing technologies, current topics in metagenomics, and the taxonomic organization of species in the Tree Of Life is given in section 3.2.

Chapter 4 provides a review about existing internal and external cluster validation techniques, the cluster validation bias and the stability of clustering results.

In chapter 5, a novel external cluster index, the Tree Index (TI), is developed to evaluate hierarchical clustering results (obtained from primary data) with respect to an external label (secondary data). In microarray data analysis, visualizations based on hierarchical agglomerative clustering results are widely applied to help biomedical researchers in generating a mental model of their data. In this context, the TI is a very helpful tool to support a selection of the to-be-applied algorithm and parameterizations.

In chapter 6, the Normalized Tree Index (NTI) is developed. It is an extension to the Tree Index and allows to identify correlated clinical parameters in microarray experiments. It runs in two steps: In the first step, a hierarchical cluster tree is obtained from the microarray data (primary data) by some hierarchical cluster algorithm. In the second step, the correlation between each clinical parameter (secondary data) and the clustered microarray data is computed by the NTI.

Visualization is a powerful tool to obtain insights into complex biomedical data. In chapter 7, a visual metaphoric display, the REEFSOM, is applied and further improved to allow the integration of clustered gene expression data (primary data) with clinical data and categorical data (secondary data) for an exploratory analysis.

The analysis of the taxonomic composition and the binning of DNA fragments of unknown species for assembly are two major challenges in current genetics. In chapter 8 hierarchical growing hyperbolic SOMs (H^2SOMs) are trained to cluster and classify small variable-length DNA fragments of 0.2 to 50 Kbp. A total of 350 prokaryotic organisms at six taxonomic ranks Superkingdom, Phylum, Class, Order, Genus, and Species in the Tree of Life are used. The hyperbolic structure of the applied SOM allows an appropri-

1.1. CHAPTER OVERVIEW

ate representation of the taxonomic DNA fragment structure and achieves reasonable binnings and classifications. DNA fragments are mapped to three different types of feature vectors based on the genomic signature: Basic features, features considering the importance of oligonucleotide patterns as well as contrast enhanced features.

The large amount of data obtained by modern sequencing technologies allows to reassess the relationship between species in the hierarchically organized Tree of Life with respect to patterns in their genomic signatures. In order to check the trustworthiness of the commonly accepted Tree of Life, its structure can be compared to the structure found by machine learning algorithms, that have exclusively been trained on DNA sequence data without using any additional information about the considered organisms. Therefore, SOMs in Euclidean and hyperbolic space are applied to genomic signatures of 350 prokaryotic organisms in chapter 9 and the structure of the signatures on the SOM grid is compared to the structure of the corresponding species in the Tree of Life.

Conclusions and final considerations can be found in chapter 10.

Chapter 2

Machine learning algorithms

Machine learning is a subfield of artificial intelligence and consolidates methods from data mining, pattern recognition, neuroinformatics, and statistics. Machine learning algorithms learn from existing data and are able to reveal hidden structures and patterns. To achieve this knowledge discovery, they require a numerical representation of objects. Based on the original measurement data, discriminable features are extracted or computed that are supposed to contain the most relevant information about the samples. These features are combined in a n-dimensional *feature vector* for each sample. The corresponding vector space is called the *feature space*. A data set is a set of feature vectors representing the objects.

Machine learning methods can be classified into unsupervised and supervised learning algorithms: In unsupervised learning, a data set $\mathcal{D} = \{\mathbf{x}_i\}$ of n m-dimensional feature vectors $\mathbf{x}_i$ is partitioned (clustered) into different groups (clusters) in such a way that the feature vectors in each cluster are as similar as possible according to some previously defined distance metric. There are three types of cluster algorithms:

1. crisp clustering (partitional clustering)

2. fuzzy clustering

3. hierarchical clustering

In crisp clustering (e.g. k-means clustering), the data set is clustered in k groups whereas k must be specified beforehand for most cluster algorithms. In fuzzy clustering (e.g. fuzzy c-means clustering) each feature vector is assigned to each of k clusters with a certain probability whereas the probabilities sum up to one for each feature vector. Hierarchical clustering (e.g. hierarchical agglomerative clustering) organizes the data in a cluster tree (dendrogram), whereas feature vectors of a high similarity are grouped close together in the same branch. The similarity between feature vectors is defined purely mathematically by a distance metric. Two most popular distance metrices are probably the Euclidean and the Pearson correlation distance metric. The Euclidean distance metric is often the first choice because of its simplicity, whereas the Pearson correlation distance metric allows to capture similar trends in the data. Hierarchical Clustering can be performed in an either *agglomerative* (bottom-up) or *divisive* (top-down) manner. By cutting a cluster tree at some level, it can be transformed to a crisp clustering result.

In supervised learning, a label or value y_i is provided for each feature vector $\mathbf{x}_i$. Besides regression, where a continuous interval-scaled value is provided for each feature vector, classification is one of the most important domains in supervised learning. In classification, a nominal label is assigned to each feature vector, indicating the class it belongs to. Based on labeled training data, the classifier *learns* to predict the label of new feature vectors, which have not been used during training. One way to classify data is to directly use the training data to assign a label to a new feature vector by considering the labels of similar feature vectors for which the label is known (e.g. k-nearest neighbor classifier). A second way for classification is to build a model from the training data that can subsequently be used to classify the new feature vectors (e.g. Support Vector Machines).

The following sections describe the machine learning algorithms used in this thesis: hierarchical agglomerative clustering, spectral clustering, Self-Organizing Maps and the k-nearest-neighbor classifier.

2.1 Hierarchical Agglomerative Clustering

Hierarchical agglomerative clustering is a favored algorithm for clustering data with an assumed hierarchical structure. The data is organized in a cluster tree whereas similar feature vectors (according to a predefined distance metric) are grouped close together in the same branch. The fact that the resulting cluster tree can directly be visualized is one reason for the high popularity of hierarchical agglomerative clustering in the domain of microarray data analysis.

In a bottom-up approach, hierarchical agglomerative clustering starts with single data points and repetitively joins the two most similar clusters until all clusters are combined in a single one (Hartigan, 1975b). In contrast to that, hierarchical divisive clustering methods follow a top-down approach by starting from a cluster containing all elements, recursively splitting each cluster into two clusters and stopping when each cluster only includes one data point.

The dissimilarity or distance between two clusters is defined as either the smallest distance of data points within the two clusters *(single linkage)*, their largest distance *(complete linkage)*, their average distance *(average linkage)*, the distance of their cluster centers *(centroid linkage)* or their inner-cluster variance *Ward linkage*. Average linkage and Ward linkage are probably the most commonly used linkage methods.

2.2 Spectral Clustering

Spectral clustering divides a data set into two clusters and can be used as a hierarchical divisive cluster method when applied recursively on the two clusters. Even though hierarchical divisive clustering follows the basic understanding of partitioning a data set, this approach is only rarely used in microarray data analysis.

Spectral Clustering algorithms focus on the analysis of eigenvectors of a *similarity (affinity) matrix* which contains the point-to-point similarities of data points. The normalized cuts algorithm (Shi and Malik, 2000), a special case of spectral clustering, favors clusters of balanced size and has the interesting property that it maximizes the inner cluster similarities and minimizes the intra cluster similarities at the same time.

Even though spectral clustering has already successfully been applied in the domain of image analysis (Shi and Malik, 2000), only few applications on microarray data can be found. Kluger et al. (2003) simultaneously cluster genes and experimental conditions, which they denote as bi-clustering. Xing and Karp (2001) use normalized cuts in combination with a feature selection process to reproduce a clustering result that is very close to the original expert labeling.

2.2.1 Normalized cuts

This section briefly summarizes the normalized cuts algorithm as described more detailed in Shi and Malik (2000):

Consider an unlabeled data set of N data points $\{\mathbf{x}_i\}, i = 1 \ldots N$ and the point-to-point similarity w_{ij} between the points $\mathbf{x}_i$ and $\mathbf{x}_j$. Upon this data a graph $\mathbf{G} = (\mathbf{V}, \mathbf{E})$ is constructed with the nodes representing the data points and the edges representing the point-to-point similarities or weights between two nodes (Figure 2.1a). The graph $\mathbf{G}$ can be cut into two disjoint parts $\mathbf{V_1}$ and $\mathbf{V_2}$ with $\mathbf{V_1} \cup \mathbf{V_2} = \mathbf{V}$ and $\mathbf{V_1} \cap \mathbf{V_2} = \emptyset$ by removing edges connecting these two parts (Figure 2.1b). The similarity between these parts can be computed as the sum of removed edges:

$$\text{edges}(\mathbf{V_1}, \mathbf{V_2}) = \sum_{i \in \mathbf{V_1}, j \in \mathbf{V_2}} w_{ij} \qquad (2.1)$$

As noticed by Wu and Leahy (1993) and Shi and Malik (2000), the minimization of equation (2.1) favors the separation of a cluster with few nodes, because the number of connecting edges increases with the number of nodes.

2.2. SPECTRAL CLUSTERING

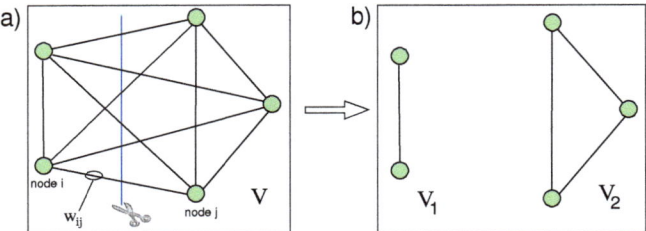

Figure 2.1: Upon the input data a graph $\mathbf{G} = (\mathbf{V}, \mathbf{E})$ is constructed with the nodes representing the data points and the edges representing the point-to-point similarities or weights w_{ij} between pairs of nodes (**a**). The graph $\mathbf{G}$ can be cut into two disjoint parts $\mathbf{V_1}$ and $\mathbf{V_2}$ by removing edges connecting these two parts (**b**).

To overcome this biased solution, Shi and Malik (2000) propose the normalized cuts (nCuts) criteria:

$$\text{nCuts}(\mathbf{V_1}, \mathbf{V_2}) = \frac{\text{edges}(\mathbf{V_1}, \mathbf{V_2})}{\text{edges}(\mathbf{V_1}, \mathbf{V})} + \frac{\text{edges}(\mathbf{V_1}, \mathbf{V_2})}{\text{edges}(\mathbf{V_2}, \mathbf{V})} \quad (2.2)$$

The minimization of equation (2.2) does not favor clusters of unbalanced size in contrast to other spectral clustering algorithms. The normalized cuts algorithm has the interesting property that it minimizes the intra-cluster similarity (equation 2.2) and maximizes the inner-cluster similarity (equation 2.4) at the same time, since

$$\text{nCuts}(\mathbf{V_1}, \mathbf{V_2}) = 2 - \text{nAssoc}(\mathbf{V_1}, \mathbf{V_2}) \quad (2.3)$$

with

$$\text{nAssoc}(\mathbf{V_1}, \mathbf{V_2}) = \frac{\text{edges}(\mathbf{V_1}, \mathbf{V_1})}{\text{edges}(\mathbf{V_1}, \mathbf{V})} + \frac{\text{edges}(\mathbf{V_2}, \mathbf{V_2})}{\text{edges}(\mathbf{V_2}, \mathbf{V})} \quad (2.4)$$

Unfortunately, this optimization problem is NP-complete because of $2^{|N|}$ possible solutions making the problem intractable for larger graphs. Nevertheless, an approximate discrete solution can be found efficiently when transforming the problem to the real value domain.

Finding the solution in the real value domain

The objective is to find the indicator vector $\mathbf{q}$ with

$$q_i = \begin{cases} 1 & \text{if } \mathbf{x}_i \in \mathbf{V_1} \\ -1 & \text{if } \mathbf{x}_i \in \mathbf{V_2} \end{cases} \quad (2.5)$$

which assigns each node (data point) to either $\mathbf{V_1}$ or $\mathbf{V_2}$. Let $\mathbf{W}$ be the matrix with the point-to-point similarities w_{ij} and $\mathbf{D}$ be a diagonal matrix, whose (i,i) entry is the sum of the entries of row i in matrix $\mathbf{W}$. It can be shown that our initial optimization problem

$$\min_{\mathbf{q}} \mathrm{nCuts}(\mathbf{q}) \tag{2.6}$$

is equivalent to

$$\min_{\mathbf{y}} \frac{\mathbf{y}^T(\mathbf{D} - \mathbf{W})\mathbf{y}}{\mathbf{y}^T\mathbf{D}\mathbf{y}} \tag{2.7}$$

with $\mathbf{y}^T\mathbf{D}\mathbf{1} = 0$ and $y_i \in \{1, -b\}$. Equation (2.7) is a *Rayleigh quotient*. If we allow y_i to take on real values, equation (2.7) can be rewritten as the generalized eigenvalue system

$$(\mathbf{D} - \mathbf{W})\mathbf{y} = \lambda \mathbf{D}\mathbf{y}. \tag{2.8}$$

The solution of equation (2.8) is a set of eigenvalues and eigenvectors. According to *Rayleigh theory*, the solution of equation (2.7) is contained in the eigenvectors corresponding to the smallest eigenvalues. Due to technical implication when dealing with nCuts, the eigenvector corresponding to the smallest eigenvalue *(Fiedler vector)* contains a trivial and non-informative solution. So the best real valued solution to our normalized cut problem is found in the eigenvector corresponding to the second smallest eigenvalue.

Extraction of the indicator vector

The final indicator vector can be derived from the eigenvector corresponding to the second smallest eigenvalue. Remember that the i-th entry of the eigenvector indicates whether data point $\mathbf{x}_i$ belongs to $\mathbf{V_1}$ or $\mathbf{V_2}$. A threshold has to be chosen such that entries of the eigenvector that are smaller than the threshold are set to -1 and the others to 1. The best way to set the optimal threshold is to

1. sort the N eigenvector entries resulting in a sorted vector $r_i, i = 1\ldots N$,

2. compute $\mathrm{nCuts}(\mathbf{V_1}, \mathbf{V_2})$ for thresholds $(r_i + r_{i+1})/2, i = 1\ldots N-1$ and

3. choose the threshold that minimizes nCuts.

It is also possible to take eigenvectors of higher eigenvalues (third, forth smallest, etc.) into account, even though they are less reliable due to their mutual orthonormal restriction (Shi and Malik, 2000).

2.2. SPECTRAL CLUSTERING

2.2.2 Future Perspectives of spectral clustering

When analyzing spectral clustering algorithms, interesting connections to other kernel-based methods from machine learning can be found which give interesting insights and sometimes lead to direct improvements of spectral clustering.

It can be shown that the nCuts approach is equivalent to *clustering with a hyperplane* (Rahimi and Recht, 2004). nCuts transform the data to a feature space and separate it with a hyperplane. This explains why nCuts are sensitive to outliers (and break elongated clusters), since they pay more attention to points away from the center. Rahimi and Recht derive an approach where each data point has uniform weight, which makes the algorithm less sensitive to outliers. They also propose a variant that only weights the data points near the separating hyperplane.

nCuts can also be seen as a special case of *weighted kernel k-means* (Dhillon et al., 2001). Knowing this, nCuts can benefit from some improvements that exist for k-means algorithms and bypass the expensive computation of eigenvectors of the affinity matrix.

Also, there is a direct equivalence between spectral clustering and *kernel PCA* (Bengio et al., 2003). Both methods are special cases of a more general learning problem: Learning the principal eigenfunction of a kernel.

Wang et al. (2005) show that there is an explicit relation between spectral clustering and *weighted kernel principal component analysis (WKPCA)*. In this way spectral clustering can also be used for feature analysis, which they call *spectral feature analysis*. This opens a wide field of application since feature selection is often a prerequisite for clustering and classification issues.

Spectral Clustering becomes computationally expensive when the number of samples increases. The same problem is faced in image segmentation, since a large number of pixels have to be processed. Charless Fowlkes et al. (2004) approaches this problem by sampling the data set and interpolating between data points.

Zelnik-Manor and Perona (2005) deal with the automatic derivation of the number of clusters and the handling of multi-scale data. They propose to use a local scale (σ_i) for each data point $\mathbf{x}_i$ and proposes a respective novel algorithm.

A *context-dependent affinity* that takes the neighborhood of data points into account is proposed by Fischer and Poland (2004) and Fischer (2005). They introduce a neighborhood size, which is less sensitive and results in a robust automatic determination of the kernel radius σ. Fischer and Poland notice that spectral clustering is merely a method for determining the block structure of the affinity matrix and propose a conductivity method that amplifies this block structure. Finally they propose to use a new *k-lines* algorithm instead of the often used k-means algorithm, when recovering the

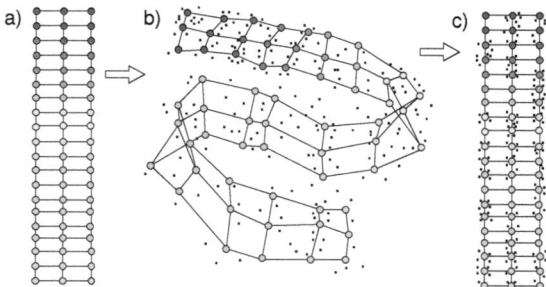

Figure 2.2: In its traditional form, the Self-Organizing Map (SOM) is a two-dimensional grid (**a**). The nodes of the SOM are adjusted by a learning rule in such a way, that the predominant data structure is captured by the grid (**b**). For visualization, the SOM grid can be mapped back to its two dimensions, and each data item can be visualized by mapping it to its best matching node (**c**).

final class assignment from the eigenvectors.
Bach and Jordan (2004) propose a complementary approach by defining a new cost function based on an error measure between a given partition and a solution from nCuts. Minimizing this cost function with respect to the partition leads to a novel spectral clustering algorithm which even allows to learn the similarity matrix from examples. Gu et al. (2001) propose a *k-way graph clustering* and *k-way bipartite graph clustering*. Ding (2002) applies spectral clustering in a recursive way as hierarchical divisive clustering and defines a stopping criteria for the recursive clustering. Yu and Shi (2003) analyse the choice of eigenvectors as generator for optimal solutions. Finally, it should be noted that spectral clustering properties need to be analyzed more intensively in the future to order to understand their performance (Weiss, 1999; Kluger et al., 2003; Fischer and Poland, 2004).

2.3 Self-Organizing Maps

Since the introduction of the Self-Organizing Map (SOM) (Kohonen, 1990), it has become a widely used tool for exploratory data analysis, visualization and classification. A SOM is an artificial neural network that allows to map high-dimensional data to a low dimensional discrete grid (the map) while trying to preserve the topology of the original data space. Even though in principle any low dimensional grid could be used, those types of maps are favored that allow a proper visualization of the projected data. The traditional and most common type of map is the two-dimensional grid (Fig-

2.3. SELF-ORGANIZING MAPS

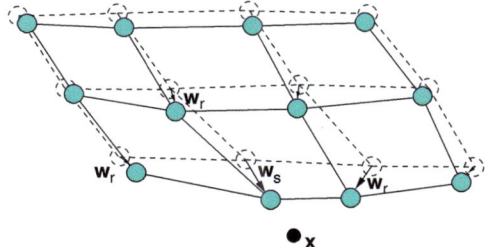

Figure 2.3: During learning, the best matching node s is determined for a randomly selected feature vector $\mathbf{x}$. The prototype vector of s, as well as its neighboring nodes are adjusted towards the selected feature vector

ure 2.2), because of its straight-forward visuability on any two-dimensional display. This and other SOM types are discussed in detail in section 2.3.1.

A training data set is required to train a SOM. Let $\mathcal{D} = \{\mathbf{x}_i\}$ be the data set consisting of n items in a m-dimensional feature space. Each node r of the SOM grid is associated with a prototype vector $\mathbf{w}_r \in \mathbb{R}^m$ in this feature space. In the standard version of the SOM, the prototype vectors are initialized with random values (a better initialization is discussed in section 2.3.1). During the learning phase, the objective is to adapt the prototype vectors in such a way that the main structure of the data set is captured and that the data can subsequently be represented by the prototype vectors. To achieve this, a feature vector $\mathbf{x} \in \mathcal{D}$ is selected randomly in each training step t. Its best matching node s is determined by

$$s = \operatorname*{argmin}_{r} \|\mathbf{w}_r - \mathbf{x}\|. \qquad (2.9)$$

The prototype vector of s, as well as those of neighboring nodes are adjusted according to

$$\Delta \mathbf{w}_r = \eta_t h(r,s)(\mathbf{x} - \mathbf{w}_r). \qquad (2.10)$$

Thereby the neighborhood function is given by

$$h(r,s) = \exp\left(-\frac{d(r,s)^2}{2\sigma_t^2}\right). \qquad (2.11)$$

It is a Gaussian shaped function centered at the winner node s, which decays with increasing node distance $d(r,s)$ on the SOM grid (Figure 2.3). The neighboring function is defined in such a way, that the prototype vector of s is adapted the most whereas adaptation decreases with distance to s on the SOM grid.

The learning rate η_t and the neighborhood size σ_t decrease continuously either in a linear or exponential way. Let η_1 be the starting learning rate and let η_T be the learning rate in the last learning step T. The linear decreasing learning rate η_t at training step t is given by

$$\eta_t = \eta_1 - \frac{t-1}{T-1}(\eta_1 - \eta_T). \qquad (2.12)$$

The corresponding exponential learning rate is defined by

$$\eta_t = \eta_1 \left(\frac{\eta_T}{\eta_1}\right)^{\frac{t-1}{T-1}} \qquad (2.13)$$

The neighborhood size σ_t is computed accordingly. In this thesis, these parameters are set as follows: $T = 10000$, $\eta_1 = 0.9$, $\eta_T = 0.1$, $\sigma_1 = 10$, and $\sigma_T = 1$.

After training is complete, any feature vector, being either from the training data set or being a novel vector, can be mapped to the SOM in feature space. Thereby each feature vector is mapped to its best matching node according to equation (2.9). Besides its mapping functionality, a SOM can also be used as a classifier by assigning a label to each node and by comparing this label to the true labels of all feature vectors that have been mapped to this node (section 2.3.2).

2.3.1 SOM types

The structure of a SOM grid has to be chosen such that it satisfies the following two conditions:

1. The topology of the original data space has to be preserved as well as possible.

2. A visualization of the SOM grid has to be possible.

Rectangular SOM

The traditional and most common type of map is the two-dimensional grid (Figure 2.2), because of its straight-forward visualibility on any two-dimensional display. Both square and rectangular grids are used. It has been shown that the SOM captures the two major dimensions of the data when mapping it to the two-dimensional grid. Therefore it is a good idea to dimension the SOM grid according to the two highest eigenvalues. The SOM nodes are initialized with respect to the two corresponding eigenvectors.

2.3. SELF-ORGANIZING MAPS

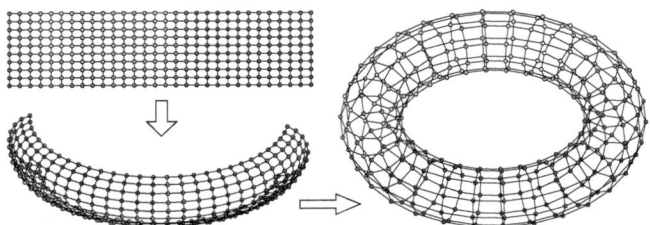

Figure 2.4: In a Torus SOM extra links are added between opposing nodes at the borders of the standard rectangular SOM. This helps to avoid "border" effects during training. By removing the extra links of the Torus SOM, it can be visualized like a standard rectangular SOM.

Torus SOM

The rectangular SOM has the inconvenient property that nodes at the border of the SOM often degenerate in feature space by focusing on outlier samples. To avoid this "border" effect, extra links are added between opposing nodes at the SOM borders to form a Torus SOM (Figure 2.4). By removing the extra links of the Torus SOM, it can be visualized like a standard rectangular SOM.

The Hyperbolic Self Organizing Map (HSOM)

A rectangular grid described in the previous sections, does not always correlate with the intrinsic structure of the data it is applied to. Especially for hierarchically structured data, an exponentionally growing display is more adequate. This property is offered by hyperbolic space. Its uniform negative curvature results in a geometry such that the size of a neighborhood around any point increases exponentially with its radius R. In a hyperbolic SOM (HSOM) this exponential scaling property has already been successfully used to visualize high dimensional text data (Ontrup and Ritter, 2005). The core idea of the HSOM is to employ a grid of nodes in the hyperbolic plane $I\!H^2$ which is then projected onto the $I\!R^2$ for inspection. The regular structure of formal nodes used by the HSOM is based on a tessellation of the hyperbolic plane with equilateral triangles (Ritter, 1999).

Hierarchically growing HSOM (H^{2}SOM)

The H^{2}SOM employs the same sort of regular lattice structure already used for the plain HSOM, but offers a hierarchically growing scheme: The H^{2}SOM is initialized with the root node of the hierarchy placed at the origin of $I\!H^2$.

18   CHAPTER 2. MACHINE LEARNING ALGORITHMS

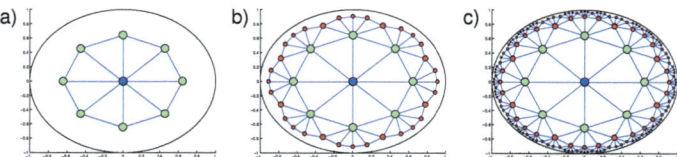

Figure 2.5: Construction of the H²SOM: The H²SOM is initialized with the root node of the hierarchy placed at the origin of $I\!H^2$. Then the n_c children nodes of the first sub hierarchy are placed equidistantly around the center node (**a**). During a first phase, the top level ring of nodes is trained in the standard self-organized fashion. After a fixed training interval, each node in the periphery is expanded as indicated in **b**). This scheme is repeated until a desired hierarchical level is reached (**c**).

Then the n_c children nodes of the first sub hierarchy are placed equidistantly around the center node as shown in Figure (2.5a). The radius of the first ring is chosen such that the hyperbolic distance of the first-level nodes to each other is the same as their distance to the center node. The *"branching" factor* n_c determines how many nodes are generated at each level and how "fast" the network is reaching out into the hyperbolic space. n_c is lower-bounded by 7 but has no upper bound (Ontrup and Ritter, 2006). During a first phase, the top level ring of nodes is trained in the standard self-organized fashion. After a fixed training interval, each node in the periphery is expanded as indicated in Figure (2.5b) and their reference vectors become fixed. In the next learning phase adaptation "moves" to the nodes of the new hierarchy level. This scheme is repeated until a desired hierarchical level is reached (Figure 2.5c). Two advantages arise from this kind of training. First, the built-up hierarchy allows a fast best match *tree search* permitting speed-ups of several orders of magnitude compared to a standard SOM or HSOM search. Second, the H²SOM forces the nodes in each ring to structure the data on different levels, i.e. hierarchies. In the first step the primary structure of the data is captured when the input data is projected to the n_c nodes of the first ring. A finer data categorization is obtained in the second step and so on.

2.3.2 SOM classifier

A SOM can be used as a classifier by assigning a label to each node, and by comparing this label to the true labels of all feature vectors that have been mapped to this node. This feature space segmentation requires a labeled training data set $\mathcal{D} = \{(\mathbf{x}_i, y_i)\}, i = 1, \ldots, N$. Each feature vector $\mathbf{x}_i$ of class $y_i \in \{1, \ldots, C\}$ is mapped to the trained SOM. To assign a label to

2.3. SELF-ORGANIZING MAPS

each SOM node, two voting schemes are presented.

Majority voting

Majority voting is the canonical way to assign a label to each node: The node label is given by the class with the majority of feature vectors mapped to that node. This voting scheme is simple but has the major drawback, that feature vectors that have been mapped to neighboring nodes are not taken into account at all. This leads to instabilities of this voting scheme. Furthermore, a label cannot be assigned to nodes to which no feature vector has been mapped. Especially for large SOMs this is a striking problem. One solution is to partition the SOM nodes into k clusters (Vesanto and Alhoneimi, 2000) at the price of introducing a new parameter k.

Gaussian weighted voting

The gaussian weighted node labeling offers a more robust way to assign a label to each SOM node. Therefore, the association of each node to each class $c \in \{1, \ldots, C\}$ is computed by summing up the gaussian weighted distances to all nodes, to which a feature vector with label c has been mapped. The association $a(r, c)$ of node r to label c is thus given by

$$a(r,c) = \sum_{i,\ c_i = c} h(r, s_i). \qquad (2.14)$$

The label n_r of node r is defined by

$$n_r = \operatorname*{argmax}_{c}\ a(r, c) \qquad (2.15)$$

In this thesis, best results have been obtained when setting the neighborhood size σ in equations (2.11) and (2.14) to $\sigma^2 = 0.5$ (chapter 8).

Classification error

The classification error e is obtained by mapping each feature vector of the testing data set to its best matching node of the trained SOM. By comparing the true class label y_i of the i-th feature vector to the label n_i of its best matching node, e can be computed by

$$e = \frac{\sum_i 1 - \delta(y_i, n_i)}{\sum_i 1}. \qquad (2.16)$$

There δ is the Kronecker delta with $\delta(i,j) = 1$ if $i = j$ and $\delta(i,j) = 0$ otherwise.

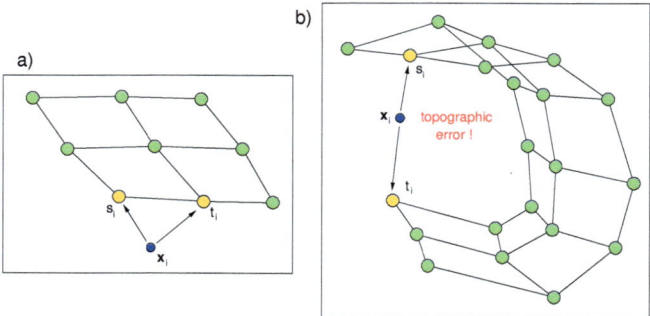

Figure 2.6: A mapping is locally topology preserving if the two nearest nodes s_i and t_i of each feature vector $\mathbf{x}_i$ are adjacent (**a**). Otherwise there is a local topographic error (**b**). The (global) topographic error is obtained by averaging the local topographic error over all feature vectors in the data set.

2.4 Topology Preservation for SOMs

For trained SOMs, several evaluation methods have been developed.

2.4.1 Topographic error

The *topographic error* $\mathcal{E}_t$ proposed by Kiviluoto (1996) is a measure for topology preservation. A mapping is locally topology preserving if the two nearest nodes of a feature vector are adjacent (Figure 2.6a), otherwise there is a local topographic error (Figure 2.6b). The (global) topographic error is obtained by averaging the local topographic error over all samples. Let s_i be the best matching node for sample $\mathbf{x}_i$ (equation 2.21) and let t_i be the second best matching node, which is given by

$$t_i = \operatorname*{argmin}_{r, r \neq s} \| \mathbf{w}_r - \mathbf{x}_i \|. \tag{2.17}$$

The topographic error $\mathcal{E}_t$ is then given by

$$\mathcal{E}_t = \frac{1}{n} \sum_{i=1}^{n} u(\mathbf{x}_i) \tag{2.18}$$

with

$$u(\mathbf{x}_i) = \begin{cases} 0 & \text{if node } s \text{ and node } t \text{ are adjacent} \\ 1 & \text{otherwise} \end{cases} \tag{2.19}$$

2.4. TOPOLOGY PRESERVATION FOR SOMS

2.4.2 Quantification error and distortion

The SOM algorithm is a vector quantization method, since it maps the data to a finite number of nodes in the feature space. The (squared) distance between an observed feature vector $\mathbf{x}_i$ and its nearest reference vector $\mathbf{w}_{s_i}$ in feature space is the (quadratic) *quantization error* (de Bodt et al., 2002). Summing up the quantization error over all feature vectors yields the *distortion D*:

$$D = \sum_{i=1}^{n} \|\mathbf{x}_i - \mathbf{w}_{s_i}\| \qquad (2.20)$$

with

$$s_i = \operatorname*{argmin}_{r} \|\mathbf{w}_r - \mathbf{x}_i\|. \qquad (2.21)$$

A low distortion indicates that the reference vectors have been positioned close to the data items in feature space. However, it should be noticed, that the distortion approaches zero in any case with a sufficient large number of SOM nodes and a sufficient small final learning rate η_T. Thus, a distortion close to zero does not necessarily indicate a high global topology preservation of the SOM.

2.4.3 Trustworthiness and Discontinuities

The SOM algorithm is a projection method, since it projects data to a lower dimensional space. To capture errors that arise in a projection, Venna and Kaski (2005) developed the measures *trustworthiness* and *discontinuities*. Trustworthiness is based on the idea that samples that are close to each other in the original data space should also be close to each other in the projected space. Let $U_k(i)$ be the set of those samples that are in the neighborhood of size k around sample i in the projected space, but not in the original data space. Furthermore, let $r(i,j)$ be the rank of sample j with respect to its distance from sample i in the original data space (Figure 2.7). The trustworthiness $M_t(k)$ is then defined by

$$M_t(k) = 1 - \frac{2}{nk(2n-3k-1)} \sum_{i=1}^{n} \sum_{j \in U_k(i)} (r(i,j) - k). \qquad (2.22)$$

The measure discontinuities is based on the contrary idea that samples that are close to each other in the projected space should have been close to each other in the original data space. Let $V_k(i)$ be the set of those samples that are in the neighborhood of size k around sample i in the original data space, but not in the projected data space. Furthermore, let $\hat{r}(i,j)$ be the rank of sample j with respect to its distance from samples i in the projected space.

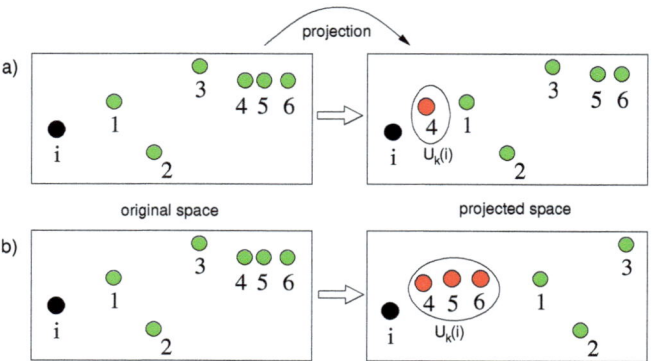

Figure 2.7: In this example, sample i has six neighboring samples. According to their distance to sample i, a rank is assigned to each neighboring node in the original space. After projection the order of the neighboring nodes might be altered. Let $U_k(i)$ be the set of those samples that are in the neighborhood of size k around sample i in the projected space, but not in the original data space. In (a), all samples except the one of rank 4 are projected correctly. Here the neighborhood size is set to $k = 3$. This leads to $U_k(i) = \{4\}$ and a trustworthiness of 5/6 for sample i. In (b), all samples in the neighborhood around sample i are misplaced after the projection. This leads to a trustworthiness of zero for sample i.

The discontinuities is then defined by

$$M_d(k) = 1 - \frac{2}{nk(2n - 3k - 1)} \sum_{i=1}^{n} \sum_{j \in V_k(i)} (\hat{r}(i,j) - k) \qquad (2.23)$$

Venna and Kaski (2005) also propose to combine trustworthiness and discontinuities to a *topology preservation index* $\hat{M}$ defined by

$$\hat{M} = (1 - \lambda)M_1(k) + \lambda M_2(k), \qquad (2.24)$$

with λ controlling the trade-off between trustworthiness and discontinuities. When applying trustworthiness and discontinuities to SOMs, different samples can have the same distance to each other on the discrete SOM grid. In this case, intermediate ranks have to be assigned to these samples.

There are two different ways to compute distances in the projected space, i.e. on the SOM grid. The canonical way to compute distances between projected samples is to compute their distance on the SOM grid. However, when applying the SOM for visualization purpose, the application of the metric as used for the visualization might be more appropriate. For the rectangular or torus SOM this metric is the Euclidean metric, since data is projected to the two-dimensional flat Euclidean space for visualization.

2.4.4 Measures based on correlations of distances

In order to check if a SOM training is topology preserving, point-to-point distances in the original space and the projected space can be compared. Let d_{ij}^1 be the distance between data points i and j in the original space, and let d_{ij}^2 be the distance between data points i and j in the projected space. For notation simplicity, let the *distance vector* $\tilde{d}_l$, $l = 1, \ldots, q$ denote all distances d_{ij}, $i \neq j$, $q = \frac{N(N-1)}{2}$, with N being the number of samples. The (linear) correlation coefficient c between the two distance vectors $\tilde{\mathbf{d}}^1$ and $\tilde{\mathbf{d}}^2$ is defined as

$$c = \frac{\sum_{l=1}^{q}(\tilde{d}_l^1 - \bar{d}^1)(\tilde{d}_l^2 - \bar{d}^2)}{\sqrt{\sum_{l=1}^{q}\left(\tilde{d}_l^1 - \bar{d}^1\right)^2}\sqrt{\sum_{l=1}^{q}\left(\tilde{d}_l^2 - \bar{d}^2\right)^2}}, \qquad (2.25)$$

with $\bar{d}$ being the mean of all $\tilde{d}_l$. The correlation coefficient c is bounded by $[-1, 1]$. $c = 1$ indicates a perfect correlation between the two distance vectors and thus a high global topology preservation, whereas $c = 0$ indicates no correlation.

A more robust measure can be obtained when ranks of distances are considered instead of the distances themselves. Bezdek and Pal (1995) apply Spearman's ρ to compute the quality of a *metric topology preserving* (MTP) transformation by computing the linear correlation coefficient of ranks of distances in the feature space and the projected space. In fact, Spearman's ρ can be used for any two distance vectors $\tilde{\mathbf{d}}^1$ and $\tilde{\mathbf{d}}^2$ when defining it as the linear correlation coefficient R_l and S_l

$$\rho_{\text{Sp}} = \frac{\sum_l (R_l - \bar{R})(S_l - \bar{S})}{\sqrt{\sum_l \left(R_l - \bar{R}\right)^2}\sqrt{\sum_l \left(S_l - \bar{S}\right)^2}}, \qquad (2.26)$$

where R_l and S_l are the ranks of the considered distance vectors $\tilde{\mathbf{d}}^1$ and $\tilde{\mathbf{d}}^2$. Spearman's ρ is a measure for the global metric preservation of a projection and is bounded by [-1,1]. A Spearman's ρ of one indicates a complete metric preservation. As ρ_{Sp} decreases from one, the projection is becoming less MTP. A Spearman's ρ of zero indicates a complete random projection in terms of distance preservation.

2.5 k-nearest neighbor classifier

The k-nearest neighbor (knn) classifier belongs to the supervised learning algorithms (Hastie et al., 2001). Because of its simplicity, it is often used as standard classifier in machine learning. The knn classifier directly uses the training data to assign a label to a new feature vector by considering the labels of the k most similar feature vectors in the training data set according to some predefined metric. A new feature vector is classified by a majority vote of its neighbors in feature space. An explicit training phase does not exist.

The parameter k specifies the number of neighbors. It can either be set by the user or it can be computed using cross-validation. In general, larger values of k make the $k$nn classifier more robust against noisiness and outliers. However, small classes become underrepresented for large k.

Chapter 3

Data

Data from two major fields of current genetics are used throughout this thesis: The first one is data from gene expression experiments. DNA microarray technology allows to measure the activity of thousands of genes for hundreds of subjects, which constitutes the primary data. The secondary data in this domain consists of clinical data and outcome for each subject. The second type of data in this thesis originates from the domain of sequence analysis. In this field, the primary data consists of DNA sequences, each sequence containing up to several millions of base pairs. In this context, the secondary data consists of taxonomic information from phylogenetics.

3.1 DNA Microarray technology

DNA microarray technology permits to simultaneously measure the expressions of thousands of genes in a tissue sample of interest. Advances of molecular methods like the polymerase chain reaction (PCR), the transcription of DNA to RNA and vice versa, the development of fluorescent dyes for labeling complementary DNA (cDNA), as well as the development of compact microarray chips let to a high-throughput technology that is applied in an increasing number of studies and is almost ubiquitous in biomedical research (Allison et al., 2006). Nowadays, the simultaneous screening of the current expression of all genes of interest allows to study diseases at their molecular level. Especially for cancer research, the application of microarray technology has become a standard tool (Perou et al., 2000; Ochs, 2003; Brennan, 2005).

A DNA microarray chip consists of thousands of tiny spots, one for each gene (Figure 3.1g). Each spot contains a high amount of a specific DNA oligonucleotide, which is a short DNA sequence and highly specific for this gene. To measure the gene expression in a sample of interest (Figure 3.1a), mRNA is extracted from this sample (Figure 3.1c). The same is done for some reference sample (Figure 3.1b and 3.1d), which consists of a mixture of normal tissue or a mixture of all analyzed tumors in cancer research. The mRNA of both the sample of interest and the reference sample is transformed to cDNA by reverse transcription. The resulting cDNAs are labeled with two different fluorescent dyes: The cDNA of the sample of interest is marked with a Cy-5 dye (red) (Figure 3.1e), whereas the cDNA of the reference sample is marked with a Cy-3 dye (green) (Figure 3.1f). The cDNAs are mixed and put on the DNA microarray chip (Figure 3.1g). Hybridization occurs in those spots where the cDNA of the sample of interest and/or the reference sample matches one of the specific DNA oligonucleotides located in the spot. All cDNA that did not hybridize is washed off the chip. An excitation with laser beams of wavelengths 670 nm (for the red dye) and 570 nm (for the green dye) indicates the amount of hybridized cDNA and can be measured by a laser scanner (Figure 3.1h). Image processing software is used to capture the amount of red and green light that is emitted from each spot on the chip. Let R_i be the amount of red light and let G_i be the amount of green light of gene i. Then the log-scaled *ratio* M_i (sample of interest to reference sample) is given by

$$M_i = \log_2 \frac{R_i}{G_i} \qquad (3.1)$$

and the log-scaled *intensity* A_i is given by

$$A_i = \log_2 \sqrt{R_i G_i}. \qquad (3.2)$$

$M_i = 0$ indicates no change in gene expression, $M_i = 1$ indicates a two-fold over-expression, $M_i = 2$ a 4-fold over-expression, whereas $M_i = -1$ indicates a two-fold under-expression, et cetera.

3.1.1 Intensity-dependent normalization

Besides many image processing and normalization challenges (Yang et al., 2002) that have to be solved, one major difficulty for obtaining unbiased gene expression ratios is its dependency on the signal intensity A. In Figure (3.2a) the ratio M_i is plotted as a function of A_i. It can be seen that M_i slightly depends on A_i. *Locally weighted scatter plot smoothing (lowess)* developed by Cleveland (1979) and Cleveland and Devlin (1988) is probably the most popular method that is used to exclude this dependency. Lowess applies a locally weighted polynomial regression at each (M_i, A_i) point in the data set. A user-defined *smoothing parameter* α determines the fraction of data that should be used to fit a local low-degree (up to quadratic) polynomial. A weight function gives more weight to points that are near the point of estimation and less weight to points that are further away. In Figure (3.2b) the lowess function is computed for the smoothing parameters $\alpha_1 = 0.05$ (red line), $\alpha_2 = 0.2$ (green line), and $\alpha_3 = 0.8$ (blue line). A high α leads to a smooth and stable regression function, whereas a small α produces a regression function that captures small fluctuations in the data.

3.1.2 Visualization

In order to get a first impression of the data, the microarray data is often clustered and visualized using hierarchical agglomerative clustering (section 2.1). Figure (3.3) displays data from the Bielefeld breast cancer project. Each square of the microarray data represents the expression of a specific gene and subject (sample) compared to reference. The gene expression is displayed with a color scale ranging from light green (high up-regulation), over dark green (low up-regulation), to black (normal expression), dark red (low down-regulation) and red (high down-regulation). The microarray data is clustered both with respect to subjects and with respect to genes (Figure 3.3a). The hierarchical clustering result is displayed as a tree on the top and on the left side of the data (Figure 3.3b and 3.3c). The rows and columns are permuted according to the leaves of the cluster trees.

In medical studies the clustered microarray data is often displayed in combination with clinical data. Clinical data that is available for the subjects is displayed between the top cluster tree and the microarray data (Figure 3.3d). It is also permuted according to the leaves of the cluster trees. Categorical data is displayed using distinct colors. Interval and ordinal data is displayed using a color scale from black (lowest value of the considered subject) to white (highest value).

3.2 Sequence and taxonomic data

Modern high-throughput sequencing technologies for DNA samples have revolutionized the field of genomics in recent years (Venter and et al., 304; McHardy et al., 2007). Nowadays, vast amounts of small DNA fragments can be sequenced at low costs using the Sanger technology (Sanger et al., 1977) and 454 Pyrosequencing (Margulies et al., 2005). Sequence assembling tools based on sophisticated computer algorithms are able to reassemble the resulting small DNA fragments to complete genomes. In the last years many organisms have already successfully been sequenced and their complete DNA sequences are stored in public databases accessible via internet (Overbeek et al., 2005). The modern sequencing technologies and the public databases containing complete DNA sequences enable, for the very first time, studies on a large number of species on a genomic level. A novel field of high interest is *metagenomics* (Handelsmann et al., 2007), which is the study of the complete genetic material directly recovered from the environment. Studies on ribosomal RNA (rRNA) indicate that traditional sequencing methods, that require a cultivation of the organisms, are unable to identify more than 1% of present prokaryotic organisms in a sample. Next generation sequencing technologies like the pyrosequencing developed by 454 Life Science bypass the step of cloning and enable to access the 99% of organisms that could not be cultured before and led to a regaining high interest in microbiology. With

Sanger technique	454 pyrosequencing
• 99.9% accuracy	• 99.5% accuracy
• slow	• fast ($\approx$100Mb/7h-run)
• expensive	• cheap ($\approx$ 8000\$ /run)
• requires cloning	• no cloning required
• creates reads of 800-1000 bp	• creates reads of 100-250 bp

Table 3.1: Advantages and disadvantages of the Sanger technique and 454 Pyrosequencing

the advent of these novel sequencing technologies, it is now possible to address the study of the complete microbial diversity of sampled communities at low costs.

Many new insights into life can be obtained when the sequence data is not studied in isolation, but when it is linked to data that is already available for the sequenced organisms. Some important information about species can be obtained from *phylogenetics*[1], which studies the evolutionary relationship between organisms in a *phylogenetic tree* (Figure 3.4), also referred to as *Tree Of Life*. However, analyses that can make use of both DNA sequences and phylogenetic information require new algorithmic approaches as it will be discussed in chapter 8 and chapter 9. This chapter focuses on the acquisition of sequence and taxonomic data.

3.2.1 DNA sequence data

The deoxyribonucleic acid (DNA) contains the genetic information that is used by all living organisms to encode proteins and their regulatory mechanisms. The sequence of the four nucleotides (adenine (A), guanine (G), cytosine (C), and thymine (T)) directly determines the encoded peptides and proteins by making use of the genetic code for transcription. Therefore, the decoding of the sequence of nucleotides is of utmost importance to gain new insights into the functioning of organisms on an intra-cellular genomic level.

In order to study biological processes on a genomic level, various biomedical methods have been developed to determine the order of nucleotides in a DNA strand. The Sanger technique (Sanger et al., 1977) is probably the most commonly applied sequencing technology. It allows to sequence genomic fragments up to 1 Kb with high accuracy (Table 3.1). However, Sanger sequencing is slow, expensive and requires cloning. A novel technology that has gained much interest in recent years is 454 pyrosequencing (Margulies et al., 2005). Even though it can only sequence DNA fragments up to 250

---

[1] *gr.*(phylon): tribe, race

3.2. SEQUENCE AND TAXONOMIC DATA

bp, it is cheap and very fast and has the major advantage that it does not rely on cloning.

Usually the sequence of an organisms consists of several millions or even billions of nucleotides. To obtain genomic fragments that are short enough to be processed by Sanger technology and 454 pyrosequencing, the complete sequence have to be truncated in several smaller pieces. Shotgun sequencing is a technique that randomly cuts (using enzymes) or shears (using mechanical forces) long DNA strands into smaller fragments of 1 Kb at the most. Both the Sanger technology and 454 pyrosequencing make use of shotgun sequencing to obtain genomic fragments that are short enough to be sequenced.

3.2.2 Sanger sequencing

The Sanger technique sequences DNA fragments with high accuracy, but with the restriction that it can only be applied on organisms that can be cultured (Table 3.1). At first, high-throughput shotgun sequencing is used to create DNA fragments of maximal 1 Kb of the target organism or organisms. These fragments are inserted into a *DNA vector* (bacterial plasmid) for amplification in *Escherichia coli* to obtain many copies of the various fragments. After purification from the bacterial cells (Fraser and Fleischmann, 1997), the amplified DNA can be sequenced using the chain termination method developed by Sanger et al. (1977) to obtain sequence reads. A sequence read is a genomic fragment up to 1 Kb for which the sequence, i.e. the nucleotides and their order, is known. In order to reconstruct the complete sequence of the original DNA strand, assembly methods have to be applied. Assembly methods make use of overlapping regions of different sequence reads to assemble them to contigs (Sterky and Lundeberg, 2000), which can then be used to reconstruct the complete sequence of the original DNA strand.

3.2.3 454 Pyrosequencing

Pyrosequencing is a novel ultra-fast sequencing technology, that can sequence whole genomes at very low costs and does not rely on cloning of the target organism (Margulies et al., 2005). It is licensed to 454 Life Science (therefore it is often referred to as *454 Pyrosequencing*), who improved pyrosequencing by using a novel parallel sequencing-by-synthesis approach to achieve the high-throughput sequencing technology of today. Single-stranded DNA of lengths up to 300 bp created by shotgun sequencing is completed to a double-stranded DNA by synthesizing the complementary strand along it, nucleotide by nucleotide. The four nucleotides (adenine, guanine, cytosine, and thymine) are repeatedly washed over the setup one after the other. Each time a nucleotide can be included in the growing complementary strand, an enzymatic reaction is triggered that causes a light signal. The high speed of the technology is due to the massively parallel processing of many single-stranded DNA fragments. The major drawback of this method is that it is limited to DNA fragments up to 300 bp, which is shorter than the DNA fragment of up to 1000 bp that can be processed by the Sanger chain termination method. However, pyrosequencing is rapidly improving and it is expected to process DNA fragments up to 500 bp in the near future.

3.2.4 Nanopores

Sequencing using nanopores is a current field of high interest in microbiology. Nanopores have the potential to sequence DNA fragments of any length. Cloning and assembling is not required, since a single DNA sequence is sufficient for the sequencing process. Nanopores are theoretically capable to sequence DNA sequences with repetitive regions. However, they have not yet left the experimental state.
Sequencing using nanopores follows a complete different approach (Fologea and et al., 2005) compared to Sanger sequencing and 454 pyrosequencing. It makes use of transmembrane proteins that have a diameter of about 1 nm. An electric potential is applied across the nanopore. Some ions pass through the nanopores and create a slight electrical current. A DNA that passes through the nanopore can only pass through it nucleotide by nucleotide. Since most of the nanopore is blocked by a nucleotide, the current that passes through the nanopore is influenced by a characteristic degree by each of the four nucleotides. The dynamic change of current flow theoretically allows to determine the order of nucleotides of the sequence that passes through the nanopore.

3.2.5 Genetic material used in this thesis

Next generation sequencing technologies like the pyrosequencing developed by 454 Life Science bypass the step of cloning and enable to access the 99% of organisms that could not be cultured before and led to a regaining high interest in microbiology. With the advent of these novel sequencing technologies, it is now possible to address the study of the complete microbial diversity of sampled communities at low costs.
With the arrival of these novel sequencing technologies that enable the sequencing of genomes at large scales at low costs, it is now possible to address issues that could not be examined before. Novel methodologies are needed to analyze the high amounts of DNA sequences in combination with supplementary knowledge about the sequenced organisms. When developing novel methodologies it is necessary to evaluate them in simulated scenarios with standardized settings and labeled data. In order to construct such a standardized scenario, sequence data from 350 different species (155 Gen-

3.2. SEQUENCE AND TAXONOMIC DATA

era, 66 Orders, 34 Classes, 18 Phyla) from either the Bacteria or Archaea superkingdom has been obtained from the public available SEED database[2,3] (Overbeek et al., 2005). This palette of species with genomes ranging from 432 Kb to 9660 Kb represents a great majority of the microbial world sequenced up-to-date. Either the complete sequences or fragments of 0.2 to 50 Kb are considered[4]. The usefulness of the approaches in the following chapters is shown on complete sequence data as well as on the large spectrum of different sequence lengths, as it occurs in metagenomic studies. Thus, the results are not biased towards the diversity of specific metagenomic samples. Nevertheless, the ultimate goal of the approaches is to apply them to real-world metagenomic data, but this is beyond the scope of this thesis.

3.2.6 Taxonomy

All existing organisms have evolved from one common ancestor according to the theory of evolution proposed by Darwin (1859). Studying the finches that inhabit the Galapagos archipelago, Darwin envisaged the fact that evolutionary forces can drive the bearing of new species from existing ones. Since then, the ultimate goal of many biologists is to obtain a hierarchical classification or taxonomy able to map the evolutionary relationships between species. Traditionally, evolutionary relationships were established using morphological characteristics (e.g. number of legs), still valid in the analysis of fossil records and in traditional taxonomy studies. The evolutionary relationship between all existing species can be modeled and visualized by the "tree like structure" which is known as the *tree of life* in science. Superkingdom, Phylum, Class, Order and Genus represent the most commonly used taxonomic categories with Superkingdom being the most general class (Figure 3.5). The complete taxonomic information of the set of species analyzed in this thesis was obtained from the taxonomy database located in the US National Center for Biotechnology Information (NCBI)[3] (Wheeler et al., 2002).

The considered 350 species are categorized on the most commonly used taxonomic ranks Superkingdom, Phylum, Class, Order, and Genus in the tree of life (3.5). On the first rank, the species are categorized in the two different superkingdoms Archaea and Bacteria. On the second rank, all species of the superkingdom Archaea are subdivided in the three phyla Crenarchaeota, Euryarchaeota and Nanoarchaeota. All species of the superkingdom Bacteria are subdivided in 15 different phyla (from Actinobacteria to Thermotogae). Finer subdivisions are obtained by the categories Class, Order, and Genus

---

[2] http://www.nmpdr.org/FIG/index.cgi
[3] This work has been performed by Naryttza N. Diaz (Center of Biotechnology, Bielefeld University.
[4] eight is the maximal number of disjunct DNA fragments of 50 Kb obtainable from the shortest genomic sequence consisting of 432 Kb

on the ranks three to five. Each genus comprises at least one species.

3.2. SEQUENCE AND TAXONOMIC DATA

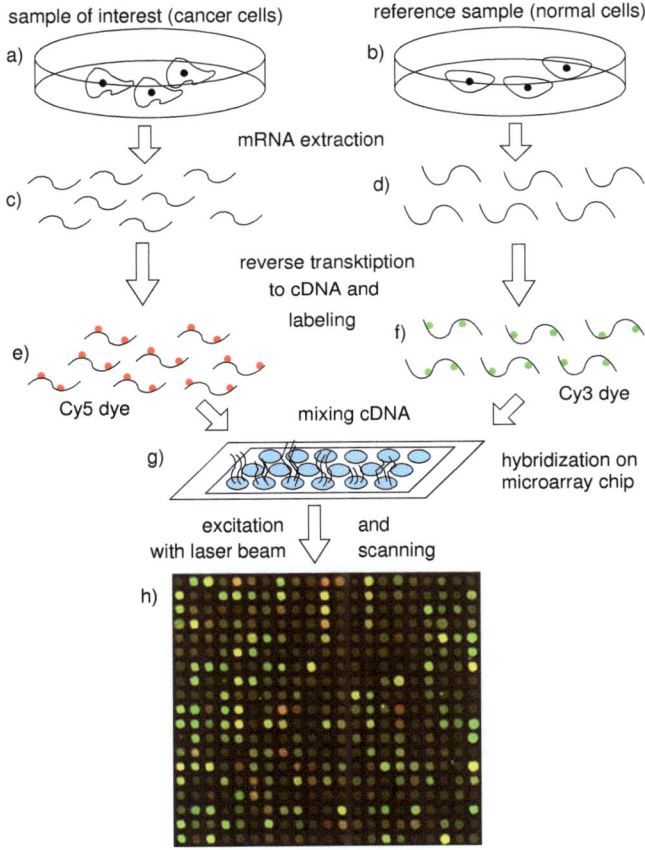

Figure 3.1: To measure the gene expression in a sample of interest (**a**), mRNA is extracted from the sample (**c**). The same is done for some reference sample (**b, d**). The extracted mRNA is transformed to cDNA by reverse transktiption. The cRNA of the sample of interest is marked with a fluorescent Cy-5 dye (**e**), whereas the cRNA of the reference sample is marked with a fluorescent Cy-3 dye (**f**). The resulting cRNA are mixed and put on the DNA microarray chip (**g**). Hybridization occurs in those spots where the cDNA matches the specific DNA oligonucleotide in the spot. All other cDNA is washed off the plate. An excitation with laser beams indicates the amount of hybridized cDNA and can be measured by a laser scanner (**h**).

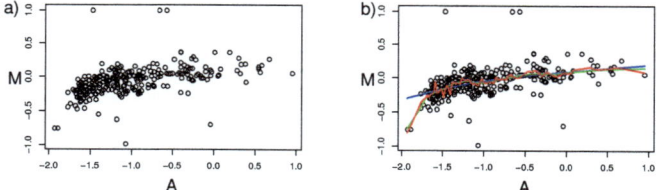

Figure 3.2: In **(a)** the ratio M_i is plotted as a function of A_i. It can be seen that M_i is slightly dependent on A_i. This dependency can be excluded using locally weighted scatter plot smoothing (lowess) **(b)**. The lowess function is computed for the smoothing parameters $\alpha_1 = 0.05$ (red line), $\alpha_2 = 0.2$ (green line), and $\alpha_3 = 0.8$ (blue line). A high α leads to a smooth and stable regression function, whereas a small α produces a regression function that captures small fluctuations in the data.

3.2. SEQUENCE AND TAXONOMIC DATA

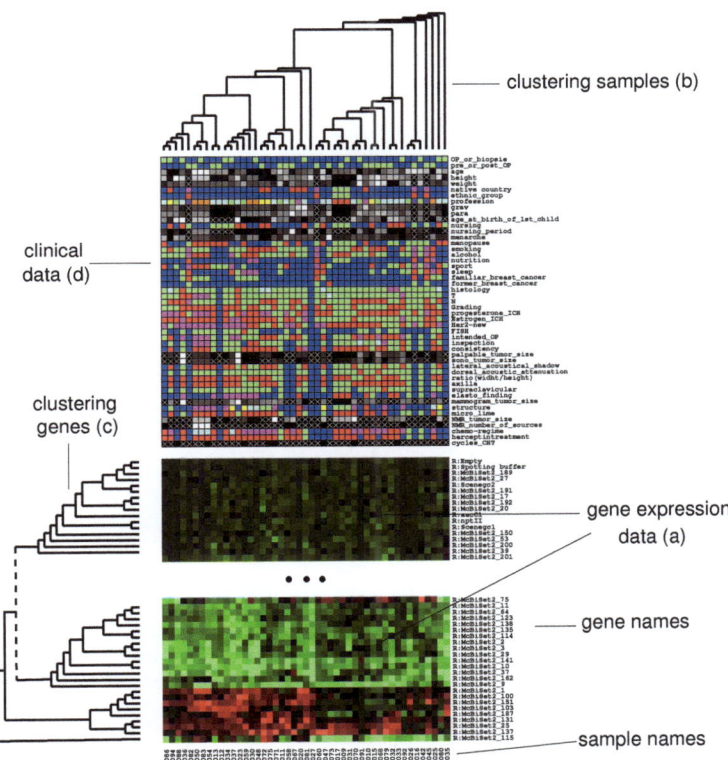

Figure 3.3: Visualization of clustered microarray data and clinical data: The gene expression data is displayed by colored squares, each one representing a specific gene and sample. A green square represents an up-regulation, a black square a normal expression and a red square a down-regulation compared to reference. The microarray data is clustered both with respect to subjects and genes (**a**). The hierarchical clustering result is displayed as a tree on the top and on the left side of the data (**b** and **c**). The rows and columns are permuted according to the leaves of the cluster trees. Clinical data that is available for the subjects is displayed between the top cluster tree and the microarray data (**d**).

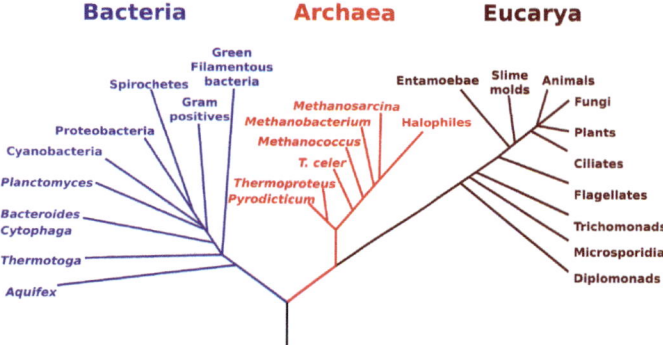

Figure 3.4: This rooted phylogenetic tree assumes that all organisms have evolutionized from one common ancestor to form the three superkingdoms Bacteria, Archaea, and Eukaryota. At the first node the superkingdom Bacteria is separated from Archaea and Eukaryota, which are subsequently separated from each other. Finer division can be observed in higher areas of the phylogenetic tree. The degree of relationship between any two organisms is directly modeled by their shortest connecting path.

3.2. SEQUENCE AND TAXONOMIC DATA					37

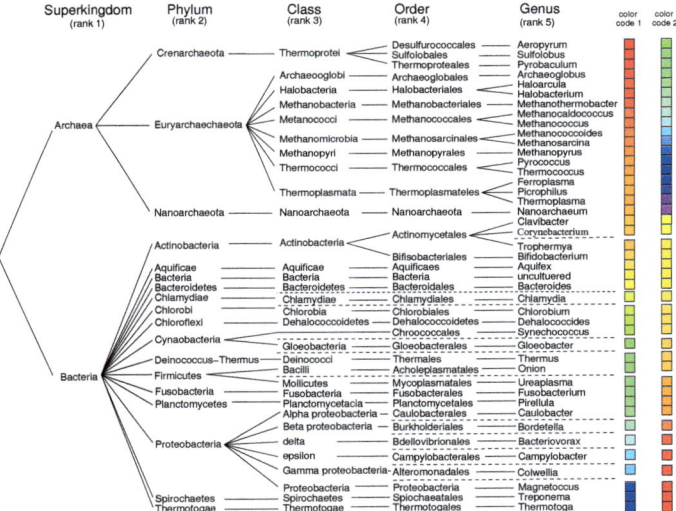

Figure 3.5: The considered 350 species of the superkingdoms Archaea and Bacteria are categorized on the most commonly used levels Superkingdom, Phylum, Class, Order, and Genus in the Tree of Life. Due to space limitations, some categories are left out in the display (dashed lines). On the first level, the species are categorized in the two different superkingdoms Archaea and Bacteria. On the second level, all species of the superkingdom Archaea are subdivided in the three phyla Crenarchaeota, Euryarchaeota and Nanoarchaeota. All species of the superkingdom Bacteria are subdivided in 15 different phyla (from Actinobacteria to Thermotogae). Finer subdivisions are obtained by the categories Class, Order, and Genus on the levels three to five. Each genus comprises at least one species. The color codes are used for visualizations in chapters 8 and 9.

Chapter 4

Cluster Validation

The analysis of novel high-dimensional complex data usually starts with the application of unsupervised cluster algorithms. These permit a first inspection into the data by revealing patterns, structures and groups that are specific for the considered data set (Duda et al., 2001; Hastie et al., 2001; Jain et al., 1999). Especially for biological data a clustering is of utmost importance, since the underlying data distribution is usually unknown, and many unexpected patterns are hidden on different levels in the data. Microarray technology has revolutionized the field of biomedical research in the last decade. Vast amounts of gene expression data are produced by an continuously increasing number of studies and experiments (Quackenbush, 2001; Ochs, 2003), confronting the researcher with the difficult task to extract the information of interest. Microarray data is usually characterized by a high dimensionality (many genes), few data points (few samples or experimental conditions), a low signal-to-noise ratio, outliers, and missing values making many standard statistical test methods applicable only to a limited extend.

When exploring this microarray data, the analysis very often includes unsupervised cluster algorithms. Unlabeled data is divided into natural groups, which may correspond to particular macroscopic phenotypes or functional categories. The cluster algorithms can be classified as hierarchical, partitioning and density-based methods (Duda et al., 2001; Hastie et al., 2001; Jain et al., 1999). Hierarchical agglomerative clustering (Hartigan, 1975b; Eisen et al., 1998; Golub and et al., 1999; Quackenbush, 2001) is the basis for most visual data mining tasks in microarray applications, since in the cluster tree (alias dendrogram) the intrinsic hierarchical cluster structure of a data set is visually accessible at once. Other traditional approaches that are well-known and are willingly taken because of their algorithmic simplicity and availability in standard software packages (Handl et al., 2005) are k-means (Tavazoie et al., 1999), fuzzy c-means (Gasch and Eisen, 2002), finite mixture models (Yeung and et al., 2001), and Self-Organizing Maps (Tamayo et al., 1999). Nevertheless, recently developed algorithms like *normalized cuts* (Shi and Malik, 2000), a *spectral clustering* approach, have also been applied to microarray data (Kluger et al., 2003; Xing and Karp, 2001). Some clustering techniques have even been developed for the explicit analysis of gene-expression data: Bi- alias coclustering simultaneously clusters samples and genes and allows to discover more coherent and meaningful clusters (Cheng and Church, 2000; Cho et al., 2004; Madeira and Oliviera, 2004). Coupled two-way clustering identifies submatrices and partitions samples and genes into biological relevant classes (Getz and et al., 2000).

Despite the diversity of the various cluster algorithms, all of them suffer from some fundamental weaknesses: Cluster algorithms do not say anything about the reliability of their produced clustering result. Even for complete random data that does not contain any structure, a clustering result is returned. The clustering result also depends on the algorithm used as well as on algorithm-specific settings. Most cluster algorithms favor partitions that are in line with their own clustering criterion, e.g. k-means clustering tends to detect spherical clusters (Azuaje, 2005). It is common practice that the estimating of the reliability of a clustering result is left to the researcher, which is a highly subjective process. Researches may overrate clusters that reinforce their own assumptions, and ignore surprising and contradictory results (Kell and Oliver, 2004; Handl et al., 2005). The subjective visual inspection alone is not sufficient to rate clustering results. It is also completely insufficient when thousand of possible clustering results generated by different algorithms and settings have to be evaluated.

Cluster indices are cluster validation techniques that provide an objective measure of a clustering result. The quality of a clustering is assessed by evaluating the data inside the clusters and by quantifying the amount of global structure captured by the clustering. Cluster indices can be grouped into *internal* and *external* ones (Halkidi et al., 2001; Handl et al., 2005). Azuaje (2005) uses the terms *statistical* and *biological*, respectively, to indicate that additional biological knowledge about the clustered data is required for an external validation.

The following overview over the most popular internal and external cluster indices is limited to crisp clustering results. This means that exactly one label is assigned to each data item. Validation techniques for fuzzy clusterings are not discussed.

4.1 Internal cluster indices

Internal indices evaluate the quality of a cluster by using only intrinsic information of the data. They use the same data which has been used by the cluster algorithm itself. To measure how well a given partitioning corresponds to the natural cluster structure of the data, many different internal

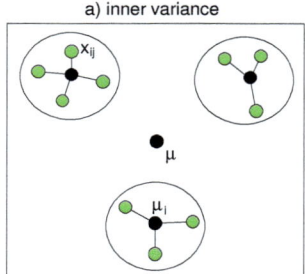 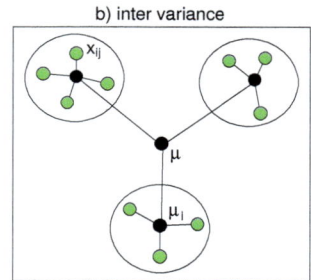

Figure 4.1: The intra-cluster variance (**a**) is a measure for the sample distances inside the clusters and the inter-cluster variance (**b**) is a measure for the distances between cluster centers.

cluster indices have been developed in the last decades. Several techniques assess both intra-cluster homogeneity and inter-cluster separation to compute a final score out of them. They are based on the fundamental principal that a good clustering result is characterized by a low *intra-cluster variance* and a high *inter-cluster variance*.

Let $\mathcal{D}$ be a data set with n elements. Let us assume, that $\mathcal{D}$ has been partitioned into k clusters by some crisp clustering algorithm (e.g. k-means clustering) Let $\mathbf{x}_i$ denote the i-th sample of the complete data set and let $\mathbf{x}_{ij}$ denote the j-th sample of the i-th cluster. Furthermore, let n_i be the number of samples in the i-th cluster, let

$$\mu_i = \frac{1}{n_i} \sum_{j=1}^{n_i} \mathbf{x}_{ij} \qquad (4.1)$$

be the center of the i-th cluster, and let

$$\mu = \frac{1}{n} \sum_{i=1}^{k} \sum_{j=1}^{n_i} \mathbf{x}_{ij} \qquad (4.2)$$

be the center of all samples.

The most popular internal cluster validity indices are summarized in the following sections. Most of these measures have already been successfully applied on microarray data (Chen et al., 2002), and are integrated in software packages for analysis of gene expression data (Bolshakova et al., 2005; Bolshakova and Azuaje, 2006)

4.1.1 intra- and inter-cluster variance

The intra-cluster variance σ_{intra} (Figure 4.1a), also referred to as *Homogeneity* (Shamir and Sharan, 2001) or cluster compactness, is a measure for the

4.1. INTERNAL CLUSTER INDICES

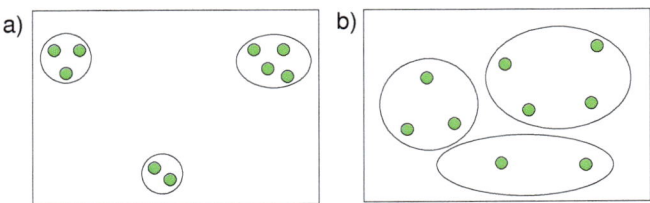

Figure 4.2: A good clustering result (**a**) is characterized by sharp clusters and a good separation, whereas a poor clustering result (**b**) is characterized by blurred clusters and a poor separation.

sample distances inside the clusters and is defined as

$$\sigma_{\text{intra}} = \frac{1}{n} \sum_{i=1}^{k} \sum_{j=1}^{n_i} \|\mathbf{x}_{ij} - \mu_i\| \quad (4.3)$$

The inter-cluster variance σ_{inter} (Figure 4.1b) of a crisp partitioning is a measure for the distances between cluster centers and is defined as

$$\sigma_{\text{inter}} = \frac{1}{k} \sum_{i=1}^{k} n_i \|\mu_i - \mu\| \quad (4.4)$$

The sum of the intra-cluster and the inter-cluster variance is constant for a data set. k-means clustering minimizes the intra-cluster variance and thus also maximizes the inter-cluster variance.

The ratio R of inter-cluster variance to intra-cluster variance

$$R = \frac{\sigma_{\text{inter}}}{\sigma_{\text{intra}}} \quad (4.5)$$

combines the two measures to a score that can be used for cluster validation. A sharp clustering result indicates a good separation and can be identified by a high R (Figure 4.2a), whereas a poor clustering result with blurred clusters is characterized by a low R (Figure 4.2b).

4.1.2 Calinski Harabasz Index

The *Calinski Harabasz Index* (Calinski and Harabasz, 1974) uses a statistical more reasonable definition of the intra and inter variance, since it takes the degrees of freedom into account.

$$\hat{\sigma}_{\text{intra}} = \frac{1}{n-k} \sum_{i=1}^{k} \sum_{j=1}^{n_i} \|\mathbf{x}_{ij} - \mu_i\| \quad (4.6)$$

$$\hat{\sigma}_{\text{inter}} = \frac{1}{k-1} \sum_{i=1}^{k} n_i \|\mu_i - \mu\| \quad (4.7)$$

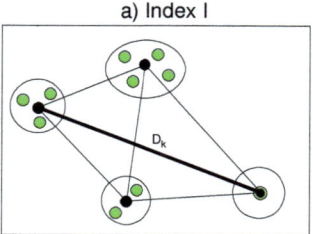 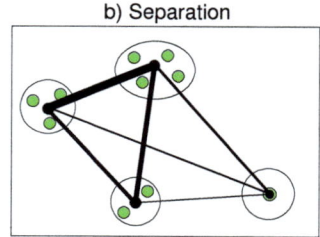

Figure 4.3: The maximal distance D_k between the cluster centers is used for normalization when computing the intra-cluster variance for the Index I (**a**). In order to compute the *Separation* of a partition, distances between any two cluster centers are weighted by the product of the number of samples in either of the both clusters (**b**). The weight is coded by the link thickness in this figure.

The Calinski Harabasz Index is then defined as

$$C = \frac{\hat{\sigma}_{\text{inter}}}{\hat{\sigma}_{\text{intra}}} \quad (4.8)$$

A high C indicates sharp clusters which are well separated from each other.

4.1.3 Index I

The *Index I* (Maulik and Bandyopadhyay, 2002) uses a different definition of the intra variance. Instead of normalizing the sum of distances by the number of samples, it is normalized by the maximal distance D_k between the cluster centers (Figure 4.3a).

$$\bar{\sigma}_{\text{intra}} = \frac{1}{D_k} \sum_{i=1}^{k} \sum_{j=1}^{n_i} \|\mathbf{x}_{ij} - \mu_i\| \quad (4.9)$$

with

$$D_k = \max_{ij} \|\mu_i - \mu_j\| \quad (4.10)$$

The Index I is then defined by

$$I = \left(\frac{\sigma_{\text{inter}}}{\bar{\sigma}_{\text{intra}}}\right)^p, \quad (4.11)$$

with p controlling the contrast.

4.1. INTERNAL CLUSTER INDICES

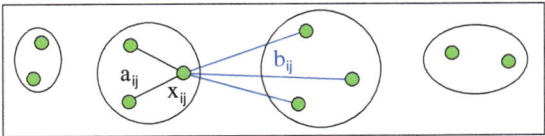

Figure 4.4: The *Silhouette Width* is based on the compactness of each cluster and on the distances to each corresponding neighboring cluster. For each data sample i, its cluster and its neighboring cluster is considered.

4.1.4 Separation

The *Separation* (Shamir and Sharan, 2001) is a measure that is closely related to the inter-cluster variance since it is based on the distances between cluster centers. Distances between any two cluster centers are weighted by the product of the number of samples in either of the both clusters (Figure 4.3b). The weighted distances are summed up and normalized.

$$\text{Separation} = \frac{1}{\sum_{i=1}^{k}\sum_{j=1,i\neq j}^{k}n_i n_j} \sum_{i=1}^{k}\sum_{j=1,i\neq j}^{k} n_i n_j \|\mu_i - \mu_j\| \quad (4.12)$$

4.1.5 Silhouette Width

The *Silhouette Width (SW)* (Rousseeuw, 1987), also referred to as *Average Silhouette* is based on the compactness of each cluster and on the distances to each corresponding neighboring cluster. For each data sample $\mathbf{x}_{ij}$, its cluster and its neighboring cluster is considered. Let a_{ij} be the average distance of data sample $\mathbf{x}_{ij}$ to all other samples in the same cluster i, and let b_{ij} be the average distance of data sample $\mathbf{x}_{ij}$ to all samples in the neighboring cluster m_i (Figure 4.4).

$$a_{ij} = \frac{1}{n_i - 1} \sum_{l=1, l\neq j}^{n_i} \|\mathbf{x}_{ij} - \mathbf{x}_{il}\| \quad (4.13)$$

$$m_i = \operatorname{argmin}_l \|\mu_i - \mu_l\| \quad (4.14)$$

$$b_{ij} = \frac{1}{n_{m_i}} \sum_{l=1}^{n_{m_i}} \|\mathbf{x}_{m_i j} - \mathbf{x}_{m_i l}\| \quad (4.15)$$

$$SW = \frac{1}{n} \sum_{i=1}^{k} \sum_{j=1}^{n_i} \frac{b_{ij} - a_{ij}}{\max\{a_{ij}, b_{ij}\}} \quad (4.16)$$

The Silhouette Width measures, for each sample, if the sample should better have been put to the neighboring cluster ($a_{ij} > b_{ij}$) or if the assignment to its actual cluster is correct ($a_{ij} < b_{ij}$). The maximal Silhouette Width is

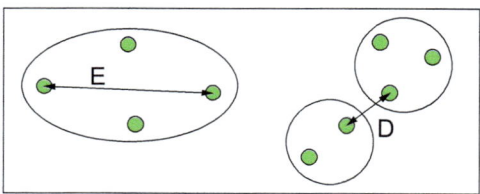

Figure 4.5: *Dunn's Index* is an index that is only based on two measures: the largest cluster expansion E and the smallest distance D between samples of different clusters.

1, indicating that each sample has been put into the correct class. The minimal possible Silhouette Width is -1, indicating that each sample should have better been assigned to the neighboring cluster.

4.1.6 Davis-Bouldin index

The *Davis-Bouldin index (DB)* (Davies and Bouldin, 1979) combines intra-cluster variances and cluster center distances in a more complex way. For each cluster i, the cluster j is searched for that has the highest (worst) ratio of the the two intra-cluster variances to the cluster center distance. These worst ratios are summed up for every cluster.

$$DB = \frac{1}{k} \sum_{i=1}^{k} \max_{j, j \neq i} \left\{ \frac{\sigma_{\text{intra},i} + \sigma_{\text{intra},j}}{\mu_i - \mu_j} \right\} \quad (4.17)$$

The lower the Davies-Bouldin index, the better the clustering result.

4.1.7 Dunn's index

Dunn's Index (DI) (Dunn, 1974) is an index that is only based on two measures: the largest cluster expansion E and the smallest distance D between samples of different clusters (Figure 4.5).

$$E = \max_{i \in \{1,\ldots,k\}} \max_{j,l \in \{1,\ldots,n_i\},\, j \neq l} \|\mathbf{x}_{ij} - \mathbf{x}_{il}\| \quad (4.18)$$

$$D = \min_{i,j \in \{1,\ldots,k\},\, i \neq j} \min_{l \in \{1,\ldots,n_i\},\, m \in \{1,\ldots,n_j\}} \|\mathbf{x}_{il} - \mathbf{x}_{jm}\| \quad (4.19)$$

$$DI = \frac{E}{D} \quad (4.20)$$

A high value of DI corresponds to a good clustering result.

4.1.8 C Index

The *C-Index* (Hubert and Schulz, 1976) considers pairs of samples in the same cluster and across clusters. Let S is the sum of distances over all those l pairs, whose two samples are in the same cluster. Furthermore, let $S_{\min}$ be the sum of the l smallest distances, when all pairs of samples - even those across clusters - are considered. $S_{\max}$ is computed in the similar way for the l largest distances. The C-index is defined as

$$C = \frac{S - S_{\min}}{S_{\max} - S_{\min}} \tag{4.21}$$

For a given data set, C is small if S is close to $S_{\min}$, indicating a good clustering result.

4.1.9 Goodman-Kruskal Index

The *Goodman-Kruskal Index* (Goodman and Kruskal, 1954; Bolshakova and Azuaje, 2005) considers all possible quadrupels of samples $\mathbf{x}_a, \mathbf{x}_b, \mathbf{x}_c$ and $\mathbf{x}_d$ in the data set. A quadruple is *concordant* if

(i) $\|\mathbf{x}_a - \mathbf{x}_b\| < \|\mathbf{x}_c - \mathbf{x}_d\|$ with $\mathbf{x}_a$ and $\mathbf{x}_b$ being in the same cluster, and $\mathbf{x}_c$ and $\mathbf{x}_d$ being in different clusters or

(ii) $\|\mathbf{x}_a - \mathbf{x}_b\| > \|\mathbf{x}_c - \mathbf{x}_d\|$ with $\mathbf{x}_a$ and $\mathbf{x}_b$ being in different clusters, and $\mathbf{x}_c$ and $\mathbf{x}_d$ being in the same cluster.

A quadruple is *discordant* if

(i) $\|\mathbf{x}_a - \mathbf{x}_b\| < \|\mathbf{x}_c - \mathbf{x}_d\|$ with $\mathbf{x}_a$ and $\mathbf{x}_b$ being in different clusters, and $\mathbf{x}_c$ and $\mathbf{x}_d$ being in the same cluster or

(ii) $\|\mathbf{x}_a - \mathbf{x}_b\| > \|\mathbf{x}_c - \mathbf{x}_d\|$ with $\mathbf{x}_a$ and $\mathbf{x}_b$ being in the same cluster, and $\mathbf{x}_c$ and $\mathbf{x}_d$ being in different clusters.

Let m_{con} be the number of concordant quadrupels and let m_{dis} be the number of discordant quadrupels. Then the Goodman-Kruskal Index GK is given by

$$GK = \frac{m_{\text{con}} - m_{\text{dis}}}{m_{\text{con}} + m_{\text{dis}}} \tag{4.22}$$

A good partitioning is characterized by many concordant quadrupels and few discordant quadrupels, resulting in a high GK.

4.2 External cluster indices

External evaluation is based on the assumption that a *real* class label or category *(gold standard)* is known for each clustered element. In contrast

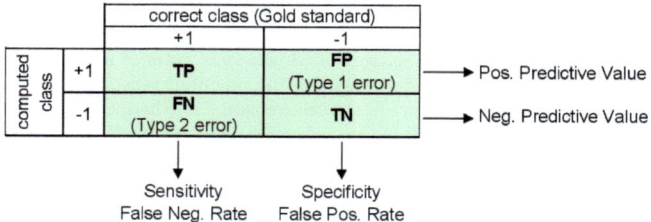

Figure 4.6: For a binary classification, the True Positives (TP) / True Negatives (TN) specify the number of samples that has been correctly classified to class one / minus one. The False Positives (FP) / False Negatives (FN) specify the number of samples that has been wrongly classified to class one / minus one. Based on the TP, TN, FP, and FN, more complex performance measures like sensitivity (Recall), specificity, Negative predictive value, Positive predictive value (Precision), False Positive Rate, and False Negative Rate can be defined.

to internal cluster indices that evaluate the quality of a clustering result by using only intrinsic information of the data, external cluster indices permit an entirely objective evaluation by making use of the knowledge of the correct class label. The clustering result which best reflects both the internal structure and the preset categories, obtains the highest score. The label can be a particular macroscopic phenotype, a functional category or any other category of interest. Thereby it is assumed that the label is somehow correlated with the clustered data. In bioinformatics, external indices have gained a remarkable popularity to evaluate results of various cluster algorithms in recent years.

In the following, let y_i denote the label of the i-th sample $\mathbf{x}_i$, and let $\mathcal{D} = \{(\mathbf{x}_i, y_i)\}$, $i = 1, \ldots, n$ be the complete data set consisting of n labeled samples.

Labels are mainly used in the field of classification: In order to measure the performance of a classifier, the computed label of each data sample is compared with the correct label (gold standard) of the sample. For a binary classification, the True Positives (TP) specify the number of samples that have been correctly classified to class one, the Tree Negatives (TN) specify the number of samples that have been correctly classified to class minus one, the False Positives (FP) (Type 1 error) specify the number of samples that have been wrongly classified to class one, and the False Negatives (FN) (Type 2 error) specify the number of samples that have been wrongly classified to class minus one (Figure 4.6). For multi-class classification of n classes, a $n \times n$ confusion matrix is used to register the number

4.2. EXTERNAL CLUSTER INDICES

of correct and incorrect classifications for each class. Based on the TP, TN, FP, and FN, more complex performance measures like sensitivity (Recall), specificity, Negative predictive value, Positive predictive value (Precision), False Positive Rate, and False Negative Rate are defined as:

$$\text{Sensitivity} = \frac{\text{TP}}{\text{TP}+\text{FN}} \quad (4.23)$$

$$\text{Specificity} = \frac{\text{TN}}{\text{TN}+\text{FP}} \quad (4.24)$$

$$\text{Negative predictive value} = \frac{\text{TN}}{\text{TN}+\text{FN}} \quad (4.25)$$

$$\text{Positive predictive value} = \frac{\text{TP}}{\text{TP}+\text{FP}} \quad (4.26)$$

$$\text{False Positive Rate} = \frac{\text{FP}}{\text{FP}+\text{TN}} = 1 - \text{Sensitivity} \quad (4.27)$$

$$\text{False Negative Rate} = \frac{\text{FN}}{\text{TP}+\text{FN}} = 1 - \text{Specificity} \quad (4.28)$$

This evaluation which is based on TP, TN, FP, and FN cannot directly be used for evaluating clustering results. In crisp clustering, the data is clustered into k groups, whereas k is not necessarily equal to the number n of real classes in the data set. Even more importantly, no specific label is assigned to the different clusters, which makes the assignment of a label to each clustered element a difficult task. Even though strategies exist that identify the most dominant class in each cluster and use this class label as gold standard, many cluster indices have been developed that directly address the problem of external cluster evaluation.

One family of external cluster indices focuses on pairs of samples. For each pair it is registered if both samples belong to the same cluster or to different clusters in the true and in the computed partition. Let m_{11} be the number of pairs $(i,j), i,j \in [1,n], i < j, i \neq j$ that are in the same cluster both in the true and the computed partition. Let m_{10} be the number of pairs that are in the same cluster in the true partition, but not in the computed partition. Let m_{01} be the number of pairs that are in different clusters in the true partition, but in the same cluster in the computed partition. And let m_{00} be the number of pairs that are in different clusters in both the true partition and the computed partition. The number of agreements is given by $m_{11} + m_{00}$, the number of disagreements is given by $m_{01} + m_{10}$, and the total number of pairs can by computed by

$$m = m_{11} + m_{01} + m_{10} + m_{00} = \binom{n}{2} \quad (4.29)$$

One of the earliest developed external cluster indices is the *Jaccard (simi-*

larity) coefficient J (Jaccard, 1908) which is defined by

$$J = \frac{m_{11}}{m_{11} + m_{10} + m_{01}}, \quad (4.30)$$

whereas a high J indicates a good clustering result.

The *Minkowski Score (MS)* (Jardine and Sibson, 1971) accounts for the number of disagreement of two partitions. In the literature it is defined as the difference between the cophenetic matrices of the true and the computed partition. For n samples, a cophenetic matrix $\mathbf{C} = (c_{ij})$ is a binary matrix of dimension $n \times n$, with $c_{ij} = 1$ if sample $\mathbf{x}_i$ and $\mathbf{y}_i$ have been clustered to the same cluster, and $c_{ij} = 0$ otherwise. Even though defined as the difference of the cophenetic matrices, the Minkowski Score can also be rewritten in terms of m_{11}, m_{01}, m_{10}, and m_{00}:

$$\text{MS} = \frac{2(m_{01} + m_{10})}{n^2}, \quad (4.31)$$

whereas a low Minkowski Score indicates a good clustering result.

The *Rand Index* R (Rand, 1971) accounts for the number of agreements of two partitions and is defined as

$$R = \frac{(m_{11} + m_{00})}{\binom{n}{2}} \quad (4.32)$$

The higher the Rand Index, the better the clustering result. Hubert (1985) developed the *adjusted Rand index*, which applies a normalization on the Rand index. It is close to 0 for random partitions and 1 for identical partitions. A further adaptation is the *weighted Rand index*, proposed and applied on microarray data (Thalamuthu et al., 2006).

In the last decade, various external indices especially for the evaluation of clustered microarray data have been proposed in the bioinformatics literature:

The *cumulative hypergeometric distribution* is used to compute a p-value measuring the probability of observing at least a certain number of genes of the same annotation in a cluster (Tavazoie et al., 1999; Toronen, 2004b). Thereby one or more functional categories can be assigned to each gene representing its biological properties. The objective to identity so-called enriched clusters, that are clusters that contain more genes of a certain functional category than one would expect in a random partition.

A *figure of merit (FOM)* is proposed by Yeung et al. (2001) to evaluate a clustering obtained by a leave-one-out cross-validation approach. The data is clustered except one sample, whose label is subsequently used as external label for validation.

4.3. CLUSTER VALIDATION BIAS

Gat-Viks et al. (2003) applies ANOVA to measure the accordance of the clustering to a linear combination of a binary vector specifying the membership to functional categories.

Datta and Datta (2006) proposes the *biological homogeneity index (BHI)* and the *biological stability index (BSI)*. The BHI measures the fraction of genes with the same annotation in one cluster and the BSI measures the stability of clustering results in a leave-one-out approach.

Finally, Steuer and Selbig (2006) uses the concept of mutual information to compare clusterings of genes. The z-score of the mutual information is used to measure to which extent the clustering result correspond to the genes' annotations.

4.3 Cluster validation bias

Ideally, a cluster index $I \in [0,1]$ should be zero for a clustering result of complete random data and one for a high-significant sharp clustering. However, most of the indices presented in section 4.1 and 4.2 do not fulfill these requirements. Cluster indices suffer from biases with respect to the number of clusters and the distribution of the cluster sizes (Halkidi et al., 2001; Handl et al., 2005).

As described in Handl et al. (2005) and Datta and Datta (2006), an adjusted cluster index can be obtained by normalizing the index with results from well-separated and random data:

Let I_0 be the expected index for random data and let $I_{\max}$ be the maximum attainable index for a sharp clustering. Similar to the computation of the adjusted Rand index (section 4.2), an adjusted cluster index I_a can be computed by:

$$I_a = \frac{I - I_0}{I_{\max} - I_0} \qquad (4.33)$$

$I_{\max}$ can usually be statistically derived, but I_0 often has to be approximated using Monte Carlo simulations: Random data sets consisting of the same number of classes and class sizes are generated under an appropriate null model. For external cluster validation, random data sets can also be obtained by permuting the external label of the data set items. I_0 is then approximated by the average cluster index computed from the clusterings of the random data sets.

4.4 Stability of clustering results

The stability and robustness of a clustering result can be estimated by repeated clustering under different conditions. The consistency of the clustering results provides an estimate of the significance of the clusters obtained. High significant clusters will not alter even if clustering conditions change.

Some cluster algorithms already have some stochastic elements incorporated in their initialization or training procedure, e.g. the k-means clustering algorithm initializes the cluster centers with randomly chosen data items and the online learning procedure of the SOM randomly selects a data item in each training step. Famili et al. (2004) applies k-means clustering and varies the number of clusters to obtain the most stable clustering result. In the absence of stochastic elements in the cluster algorithm, the stability and robustness of a clustering result can be assessed by

1. subsampling the original data set (bootstrapping) or by
2. perturbating the original data.

Levine and Domany (2001), Kerr and Churchill (2001), Hur et al. (2002), and Dudoit and Fridlyand (2002) draw subsamples in a bootstrapping approach to assess the stability of clustering results. Smolkin and Ghosh (2003) compares a clustering result to a predefined clustering and computes a stability score using the technique proposed by Hur et al. (2002). Bittner et al. (2000) applies the second approach and adds Gaussian distributed noise in the range of experimental noise to the original data. To guarantee that the biological noise is stronger than the added noise, the amount of noise is estimated from the gene expression data. An alternative way for assessing cluster validity is to summarize clustering results obtained by different cluster algorithms and different settings (consensus clustering) in a cophenetic matrix Romesburg (1984).

Chapter 5

The Tree Index

The last chapter reviewed the most popular internal and external cluster indices for clustering results. A drawback of those indices is that they all work on results obtained by partitioning methods. The data must be clustered in k groups, whereas k must either be estimated beforehand or during the cluster evaluation process. Hierarchical cluster trees are usually evaluated by cutting the tree at some level yielding k clusters. Even though an evaluation of a hierarchical cluster tree applying traditional indices (for partitions) at any level of the tree is imaginable, the development of a stable and unbiased index for trees is not straight-forward. *Random tree models* assume that all possible rooted trees based on n objects are equally likely. Gordon (1980) reviews several models that have been developed and suggests to use them as null models to assess the validity of hierarchical classifications. However, limitations of null models are also reported in his book and applications on real-world data are not available. Toronen (2004b) considers each split in a hierarchical cluster tree and uses the cumulative hypergeometric distribution to identify the split that lead to the strongest functional enrichment in a cluster. The functional enrichment is defined as the percentage of genes in a cluster that belongs to the same previously defined functional category. The cluster with strongest functional enrichment is marked as Best Scoring Cluster (Toronen, 2004a).

During my PhD, I developed a novel external cluster index for hierarchical cluster trees, the *Tree Index (TI)*. Since then, the TI has proven its usability in two major biomedical issues: As stated in chapter 4, hierarchical agglomerative clustering is the basis for most visual data mining tasks in microarray applications, since in a cluster tree the intrinsic hierarchical cluster structure of a data set is visually accessible at once. One problem in this clustering based exploratory data analysis is the variability of the clustering result dependent on the applied cluster algorithm and parameterizations (preprocessing of the data, (dis-)similarity measure). There is hardly any consensus about how to choose these (Handl et al., 2005;

Gat-Viks et al., 2003). This results in an enormous number of potential visual displays for one data set (section 5.3.1) leading to the confusion of the biomedical researcher. It is common practice to test different algorithms and parameterizations and to select the clustering result which seems to be the most appropriate according to one's knowledge and anticipations. Thus, an analytical and objective evaluation of clustering results would help to identify the algorithm and parameterization that yield objectively reasonable clustering results. The TI can be used to identify the algorithm and parameterization (preprocessing of the data, (dis-)similarity measure), yielding the clustering that is best suited for visualization. In biomedical applications, microarray data is usually analyzed in combination with additional variables, like clinical data or tumor classifications. Thus we measure the usefulness of a tree visualization according to an external class label. For demonstration, the index is applied on cluster trees created by agglomerative clustering and normalized cuts on simulated data as well as on two public available cancer data sets.

The second major field of application of the TI is to use it for the identification of external labels (e.g. clinical variables) that are highly correlated with the clustered data (e.g. microarray data). This application will be discussed in chapter 6.

5.1 Methods

We consider a preprocessed microarray data set with d samples (for instance derived from d tissue samples) of g genes, $\mathcal{X} = \{\mathbf{x}_1, \ldots, \mathbf{x}_i, \ldots, \mathbf{x}_d\}, \dim \mathbf{x}_i = g$. Based on some background information, one out of κ possible external labels or categories $c_i \in \{\mathcal{C}_1, \ldots, \mathcal{C}_\kappa\}$ is assigned to each sample $\mathbf{x}_i$ (for instance $\mathcal{C}_j$ = tumor classification of the tissue). In contrast to classification, we use the data labels to tune our visualization and not to predict a class for a new sample. Let us now assume that $\mathcal{X}$ has been clustered by some hierarchical agglomerative or divisive cluster algorithm yielding a cluster tree (Figure 5.1). To characterize the features of a cluster tree, that allow efficient visual data mining, we consider the tree as a result of a statistical process. In the ideal case, the data is divided into homogeneous clusters at the first split (Figure 5.1a). Usually such an optimal cluster tree cannot be generated for real data. In a more realistic scenario an appealing cluster tree is characterized by many splits that divide a heterogeneous clusters into nearly homogeneous subclusters (Figure 5.1b). The purer and larger the subclusters in a split, the more interesting they are, since each of them is defined by a clear pattern of variables that separate it from the rest of the data. Cluster trees with heterogeneous subclusters (Figure 5.1c) or degenerated cluster trees (Figure 5.1d) separating only single elements from the rest of the data in each split are of lower visual quality. When considering

5.1. METHODS

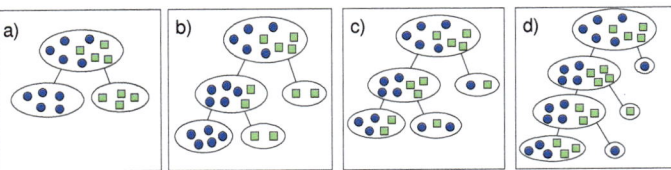

Figure 5.1: Characteristics of appealing and non-appealing cluster trees: The first splits of four different cluster trees are shown. In an optimal cluster tree the data is divided into homogeneous clusters at the very first split (**a**). Usually such an optimal cluster tree cannot be generated for real data. An appealing cluster tree is rather characterized by many (here: two) splits inside the cluster tree each dividing a heterogeneous cluster into almost homogeneous subclusters (**b**). The purer and larger the subclusters in a split, the cluster tree is well (**b**) or not well (**c**) suited for a visual datamining task. A degenerated cluster tree (**d**) separating only single elements from the rest of the data in each split if of a lower quality.

the splits of a cluster tree from a statistical point of view, the probabilities of the splits permit to distinguish between cluster trees of different qualities. Obviously, a cluster tree of high quality is characterized by many unlikely splits, separating large homogeneous clusters from the rest of the data.

We now introduce the *Tree Index*, which is based on the evaluation of probabilities of every single split in a cluster tree. Clusters, also homogeneous ones, are always split until only singleton clusters are left since the label is not considered during the clustering process (Figure 5.2). In a first step a *splitting score* is computed for every single split in the cluster tree based on the probability of the split. In a second step, all splitting scores are combined to compute the final Tree Index.

Step 1: Looking at the r-th split (the splits are numbered arbitrary), a cluster with N elements is split into l (usually $l = 2$) smaller subclusters (Figure 5.2). The elements of the main cluster belong to κ different categories whereas $n_\lambda, \lambda \in \{1, \ldots, \kappa\}$ specifies the number of elements belonging to category $\mathcal{C}_\lambda$. The i-th subcluster contains m_i elements with $m_{i\lambda}$ elements belonging to category $\mathcal{C}_\lambda$. The primary objective is to compute the probability of such a particular split by taking the observed distributions in the clusters into account. It is assumed that $m_i, i \in \{1, \ldots, l\}$ elements are drawn from the N elements by sampling without replacement. Thereby each element is drawn with the same probability. For two categories ($\kappa = 2$) and two subclusters ($l = 2$) the probability of the observed distribution is

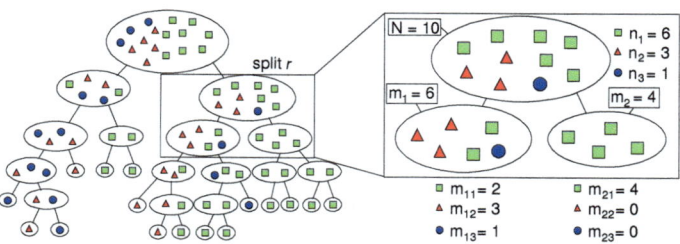

Figure 5.2: Inspection of one single split: In the r-th split, a cluster with $N = 10$ elements belonging to $\kappa = 3$ categories is split into $l = 2$ subclusters, each containing m_i elements with $m_{i\lambda}$ elements belonging to category $\mathcal{C}_\lambda$. In this split a completely homogeneous cluster is separated from the rest of the data. From a statistical point of view this event is rather unlikely resulting in a high splitting score for the r-th split.

given by the *hypergeometric distribution*.

$$p(m_{11}, m_{12}; N, n_1, m_1, m_2) = \frac{\binom{m_1}{m_{11}}\binom{m_2}{m_{12}}}{\binom{N}{n_1}} \quad (5.1)$$

with $m_{11} + m_{12} = n_1$ and $m_1 + m_2 = N$. For $m_{11} \in [0, 100]$, $N = 500$, $n_1 = 200$, and $m_1 = 100$, the hyperbolic distribution is plotted in Figure (5.4).
For the general case (κ categories and l subclusters) the probability is given by a generalized form of the *polyhypergeometric distribution* or *multivariate hypergeometric distribution* (Johnson et al., 1997). Let $\mathbf{M} = \{m_{i\lambda}\}$, $\mathbf{n} = \{n_\lambda\}$, and $\mathbf{m} = \{m_i\}$ with $1 \leq i \leq l$ and $1 \leq \lambda \leq \kappa$.

$$p(\mathbf{M}; N, \mathbf{n}, \mathbf{m}) = \frac{\prod_{i=1}^{l} \frac{m_i!}{\prod_{\lambda=1}^{\kappa} m_{i\lambda}!}}{\frac{N!}{\prod_{\lambda=1}^{\kappa} n_\lambda!}} \quad (5.2)$$

$p(\mathbf{M}; N, \mathbf{n}, \mathbf{m})$ decreases with the size of the cluster that is split and with the homogeneity of the subclusters. The probability reaches its maximum if the distribution in a given cluster correlates to the distribution in the subcluster, indicating a random split. We define the splitting score S_r of the r-th split by its negative logarithmic probability.

$$\begin{aligned} S_r(\mathbf{M}; N, \mathbf{n}, \mathbf{m}) &= -\ln p(\mathbf{M}; N, \mathbf{n}, \mathbf{m}) \\ &= \ln N! - \sum_{\lambda=1}^{\kappa} \ln n_\lambda! - \sum_{i=1}^{l}\left(\ln m_i! - \sum_{\lambda=1}^{\kappa} \ln m_{i\lambda}!\right) \end{aligned} \quad (5.3)$$

5.1. METHODS

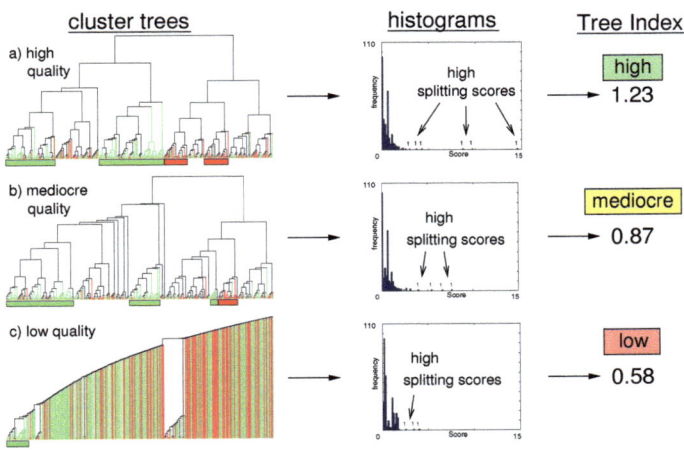

Figure 5.3: Cluster trees and histograms with a high (obtained by spectral clustering, $\sigma = 10^{-2}$, euclidean (dis-)similarity, all normalization), mediocre (obtained by complete linkage, $\sigma = 1$, eucl., all norm.), and low (obtained by single linkage, $\sigma = 1$, eucl., all norm.) Tree Index (TI) are shown. In all histograms, many splitting scores are close to zero. These result from less important splits dividing small clusters. The quantity and amplitude of a few high splitting scores characterize the quality of a cluster tree. A cluster tree with a high TI is characterized by a histogram with some splitting scores of high amplitude (a). These splitting scores correspond to splits inside the cluster tree that divide clusters in large and nearly pure subclusters. A cluster tree with a mediocre TI is characterized by a histogram with some splitting scores of a middle amplitude (b). These splitting scores correspond to less important splits inside the cluster tree that divide clusters in less larger and less purer subclusters than observed in the cluster tree with the high TI. A cluster tree with a low TI is characterized by only a very few splitting scores of low amplitude (c). Such a degenerated cluster tree consists of many splits separating only one single element from the rest of the data.

A splitting score of a given cluster reaches its minimum if the distribution in the cluster correlates to the distribution in the subclusters. The splitting score increases with the size of the cluster that is split and with the homogeneity of the subclusters. Thus splits at higher levels in a cluster tree dividing larger clusters are generally capable to produce higher splitting scores. Splits at lower levels in a cluster tree divide clusters containing

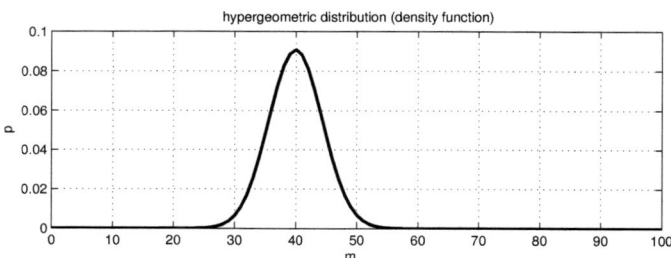

Figure 5.4: This *hypergeometric distribution* function describes the probability to observe $m_{11} \in [0, 100]$ elements of category $\mathcal{C}_1$ in a cluster of size $m_1 = 100$, when there is a total of $N = 500$ elements, with $n_1 = 200$ elements of category $\mathcal{C}_1$.

only few elements. This results in many splitting scores close to zero, since most of the splits are located in the lower part of a cluster tree. A split dividing a homogeneous cluster always has a splitting score of zero. Therefore the splits inside homogeneous clusters are of no importance for the further computation of the Tree Index.

Step 2: The set of all splitting scores enables to distinguish between cluster trees of different qualities. Independent of the internal structure of the cluster tree, the sum of all splitting scores is constant. Many splitting scores are zero (splits of homogeneous clusters) or close to zero (splits of small clusters). For illustration cluster trees of a high, mediocre and low quality are presented in Figure (5.3).

A cluster tree of low quality is characterized by mostly low splitting scores and a very few high splitting scores (Figure 5.3c). A cluster tree of high quality has considerably more high splitting scores (Figure 5.3a).

To combine the complete set of splitting scores to a parameter-free index, we propose to use the standard deviation of splitting scores to capture the quality of a cluster tree, by defining the Tree Index (TI) by:

$$\text{TI} = \sqrt{\frac{1}{R} \sum_{r=1}^{R} \left(S_r - \bar{S} \right)^2}, \text{ with } \bar{S} = \frac{1}{R} \sum_{r=1}^{R} S_r, \qquad (5.4)$$

and R the number of splits in the cluster tree. $\bar{S}$ is close to zero because at least those half of the S_r are close to zero, that belong to splits at the lowest level of the cluster tree. Thus, the quantity and amplitude of high S_r basically determines the index. The higher the index, the more appealing is the corresponding cluster tree display.

5.2 Results

For illustration, the Tree Index is applied on cluster trees obtained from simulated data and two public available cancer data sets.

5.2.1 Simulated data

Our artificial data set $\mathcal{C}$ consists of five classes, each containing eight items that are scattered around their class centers with normally distributed noise ($\sigma^* = 0.1$):

$$\mathcal{C} = \bigcup_{i=1}^{5} \mathcal{C}_i, \text{ with } \mathcal{C}_i = \{(\mathbf{x}_j, c_j), \mathbf{x}_j \in \mathcal{N}(\mu_i, \sigma^*), c_j = i, j \in [1,8]\}, \quad (5.5)$$

whereas $(\mathbf{x}_j, c_j)$ comprises a two-dimensional data point $\mathbf{x}_j$ and the corresponding label c_j. The class centers are given by $\mu_1 = (2,2)^T$, $\mu_2 = (5,2)^T$, $\mu_3 = (3,10)^T$, $\mu_4 = (50,2)^T$, and $\mu_5 = (50,4)^T$, meaning that $\mathcal{C}_1$ and $\mathcal{C}_2$ as well as $\mathcal{C}_4$ and $\mathcal{C}_5$ are grouped close together, with a large gap between the two groups, whereas $\mathcal{C}_3$ is located in the further vicinity of $\mathcal{C}_1$ and $\mathcal{C}_2$. Now, additional normally distributed noise $\sigma \in [0.1, 100]$ is added to each point in the data set $\mathcal{C}$ to create a perturbated data set $\mathcal{D}_\sigma$:

$$\mathcal{D}_\sigma = \{(\mathbf{x}_j + \eta_j, c_j), \mathbf{x}_j \in \mathcal{C}, \eta_j \in \mathcal{N}(0, \sigma)\} \quad (5.6)$$

Four such data sets $\mathcal{D}_{0.1}$, $\mathcal{D}_{1.12}$, $\mathcal{D}_{6.32}$, and $\mathcal{D}_{89.1}$ are shown in Figure (5.5a). Their corresponding hierarchical clustering results are displayed below (Figure 5.5b). In Figure (5.5b$_1$) the five classes are well separated. In a first step, the items of each class are grouped together (i). Then the classes $\mathcal{C}_1$ and $\mathcal{C}_2$ (ii) as well as $\mathcal{C}_4$ and $\mathcal{C}_5$ (iii) are linked to each other, followed by $\mathcal{C}_3$ that is linked to $\mathcal{C}_1$ and $\mathcal{C}_2$ (iv). As noise increases, $\mathcal{C}_1$ and $\mathcal{C}_2$ (v) as well as $\mathcal{C}_4$ and $\mathcal{C}_5$ (vi) cannot be separated any more by the cluster algorithm (Figure 5.5b$_2$). With a further increase of noise, $\mathcal{C}_3$ (vii) melts with $\mathcal{C}_1$ and $\mathcal{C}_2$ (Figure 5.5b$_3$), but $\mathcal{C}_1, \mathcal{C}_2$ and $\mathcal{C}_3$ are still separated from $\mathcal{C}_4$ and $\mathcal{C}_5$ (viii). Finally, with very high noise, an identification of the original classes is not possible any more (Figure 5.5b$_4$).

Figure (5.5c) displays the corresponding scores of the four experiments. It can be seen, that the number of high splitting scores decreases as noise increases.

The four experiments of Figures (5.5a) to (5.5c) are integrated in Figure (5.5d), where for each σ, the experiment is repeated 50 times, and the computed TIs are displayed in Box-and-Whisker plots. Obviously, the TI decreases as noise increases. (ix) marks the position of the perfect separation of the clusters, (x) the position where $\mathcal{C}_1$ and $\mathcal{C}_2$ as well as $\mathcal{C}_4$ and $\mathcal{C}_5$ are combined in one cluster. (xi) marks the position where $\mathcal{C}_3$ cannot be separated from $\mathcal{C}_1$ and $\mathcal{C}_2$ any more and (xii) indicates a complete random clustering.

The fact that the TI decreases as noise increases makes the TI a reliable index to measure how well the label is reflecting the structure of the clustered data and how well a specific cluster tree is suited for visualization.

5.2.2 Real-world Cancer data sets

By applying the TI on real-world data sets, we simulate the scenario where a biomedical researcher is looking for the most appropriate algorithm and parameterization to visualize the cluster structure in the data.

The first data set is the breast cancer data set of van de Vijver et al. (2002) [1] which is an extension to the study of van't Veer et al. (2002) and one of the most extensive and informative studies performed to date. For each of the 295 subjects in the study, 24496 genes are analyzed and clinical data as well as outcome is available. In our study the clustering of subjects is performed on logarithms of ratios of a set of 231 marker genes identified by van't Veer et al. (2002). The logarithms are either scaled to $[-1, 1]$ (all normalization) or they are scaled separately to $[-1, 1]$ for each gene (single gene normalization). The data is separated into two classes of those tumors that develop metastasis and those which do not. We use this information as the external label (C_i) since the user seeks for groups of cases that have a similar genetic profile and are of the same tumor class.

The second data set is the multi-class cancer data set of Ramaswamy et al. (2001) containing 288 subjects and 16063 genes. The data is separated into 22 different cancer types that are taken as external labels ($C_0, \ldots, C_{21}$). Thereby it is assumed that there is a correlation between the cancer type and the microarray data.

In order to create a large range of possible tree visualizations, two different preprocessings are applied (all and single gene normalization), and two different (dis-)similarity measures with five different scaling factors (see next paragraph) are used. The data set is clustered by the normalized cuts algorithm (Shi and Malik, 2000) applied in a hierarchical manner and by five variants of hierarchical agglomerative clustering (single linkage, complete linkage, average linkage, Centroid, Ward). This results in a total of $2 \times 2 \times 5 \times 6 = 120$ cluster results. The cluster tree with the highest Tree Index is selected for final visualization.

Similarity and dissimilarity measures

Both the Euclidean distance and the Pearson correlation coefficient are used with a scaling factor specifying the sensitivity of the measures. The normalized cuts algorithm requires a similarity measure $w_{ij} \in [0, 1]$ of two expression profiles $\mathbf{x}_i$ and $\mathbf{x}_j$ of dimension g whereas hierarchical agglomerative

---

[1] downloadable at http://www.rii.com/publications/2002/nejm.html

5.2. RESULTS

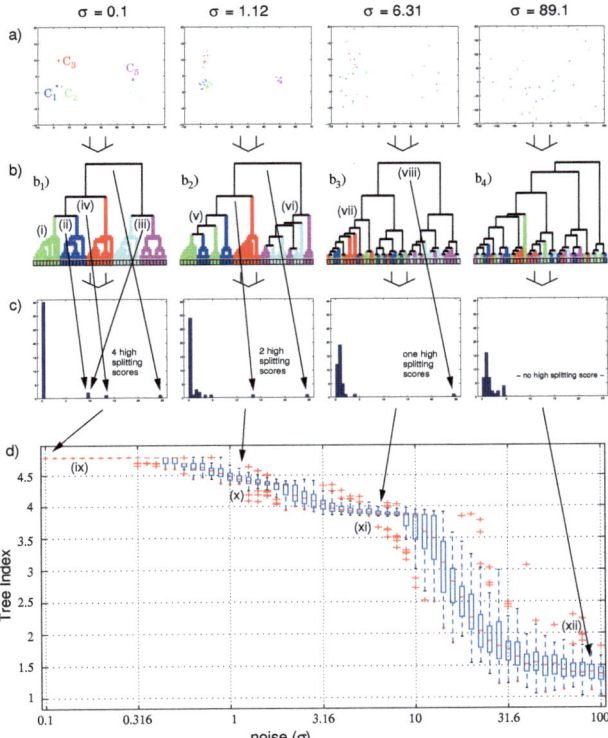

Figure 5.5: Four perturbated data sets $\mathcal{D}_{0.1}$, $\mathcal{D}_{1.12}$, $\mathcal{D}_{6.32}$, and $\mathcal{D}_{89.1}$ are shown in **a)**. Their corresponding hierarchical clustering results are displayed below (**b**). In (**b**$_1$) the five classes are well separated. In a first step, the items of each class are grouped together (i). Then the classes $\mathcal{C}_1$ and $\mathcal{C}_2$ (ii) as well as $\mathcal{C}_4$ and $\mathcal{C}_5$ (iii) are linked to each other, followed by $\mathcal{C}_3$ that is linked to $\mathcal{C}_1$ and $\mathcal{C}_2$ (iv). As noise increases, $\mathcal{C}_1$ and $\mathcal{C}_2$ (v) as well as $\mathcal{C}_4$ and $\mathcal{C}_5$ (vi) cannot be separated any more by the cluster algorithm (**b**$_2$). With a further increase of noise, $\mathcal{C}_3$ (vii) melts with $\mathcal{C}_1$ and $\mathcal{C}_2$ (**b**$_3$), but $\mathcal{C}_1, \mathcal{C}_2$ and $\mathcal{C}_3$ are still separated from $\mathcal{C}_4$ and $\mathcal{C}_5$ (viii). Finally, with very high noise, an identification of the original classes is not possible any more (**b**$_4$). (**c**) displays the corresponding scores of the four experiments. It can be seen, that the number of high splitting scores decreases as noise increases. The four experiments of (**a**) to (**c**) are integrated in (**d**), where for each σ, the experiment is repeated 50 times, and the computed TIs are displayed in Box-and-Whisker plots. Obviously, the TI decreases as noise increases. (ix) marks the position of the perfect separation of the clusters, (x) the position where $\mathcal{C}_1$ and $\mathcal{C}_2$ as well as $\mathcal{C}_4$ and $\mathcal{C}_5$ are combined in one cluster. (xi) marks the position where $\mathcal{C}_3$ cannot be separated from $\mathcal{C}_1$ and $\mathcal{C}_2$ any more and (xii) indicates a complete random clustering.

clustering requires a dissimilarity measure $d_{ij} \in [0,1]$. For our studies we apply $d_{ij} = 1 - w_{ij}$. The first similarity measure is defined as

$$w_{ij} = \exp\left\{-\frac{\mu(\mathbf{x}_i, \mathbf{x}_j)}{\sigma g}\right\}, \text{ with } \mu(\mathbf{x}_i, \mathbf{x}_j) = \sqrt{\sum_{k=1}^{g}(x_{ik} - x_{jk})^2}$$

and scaling factor σ. The second similarity measure is based on the Pearson correlation coefficient (Ochs, 2003), which corresponds to the intuitive understanding of correlation and is often used in the domain of microarray data analysis (Eisen et al., 1998; Xing and Karp, 2001). It is defined as

$$w_{ij} = \exp\left\{-\frac{1 - \rho(\mathbf{x}_i, \mathbf{x}_j)}{\sigma}\right\}, \text{ with } \rho(\mathbf{x}_i, \mathbf{x}_j) = \frac{1}{g}\sum_{k=1}^{g}\left(\frac{x_{ik} - \bar{\mathbf{x}}_i}{s_i}\right)\left(\frac{x_{jk} - \bar{\mathbf{x}}_j}{s_j}\right)$$

where $\bar{x}_i = \frac{1}{g}\sum_{k=1}^{g} x_{ik}$ and $s_i = \sqrt{\frac{1}{g}\sum_{k=1}^{g}(x_{ik} - \bar{x}_i)^2}$. In our study we use five different scaling factors $\sigma \in \{10^{-3}, 10^{-2}, 0.1, 1, 10\}$.

Results

Breast cancer data set (van de Vijver) Results of the van de Vijver breast cancer data set are displayed in Figure (5.6). The highest Tree Index is obtained for complete linkage clustering, the correlation dissimilarity measure, all normalization, and a scaling factor of 10. In the cluster tree, the subjects are colored according to their category (metastasis or no metastasis). It can be seen that in the very first split the data has been separated in an nearly homogeneous cluster (many subjects without metastasis) and a heterogeneous cluster. Such a split obtains a high splitting score and increases the Tree Index considerably.

In Figure (5.7) the tree indices obtained for the van Vijver data set are presented again, but a cluster tree of a mediocre quality is selected this time. It can be seen that the data is not that good separated according to its external label. In many splits only single elements are separated from the rest of the data. Consequently this leads to a less appealing visualization and a lower Tree Index.

Multi-class cancer data set (Ramaswamy) Results of the Ramaswamy data set are displayed in Figure (5.8). The highest Tree Index is obtained for Ward clustering, the correlation dissimilarity measure, all normalization, and a scaling factor of 0.1. In the cluster tree, the subjects are colored according to their category (tumor type). Additionally, homogeneous clusters containing two or more elements are labeled with letters. It can be seen that in various splits, homogeneous clusters are separated from the rest of

5.2. RESULTS

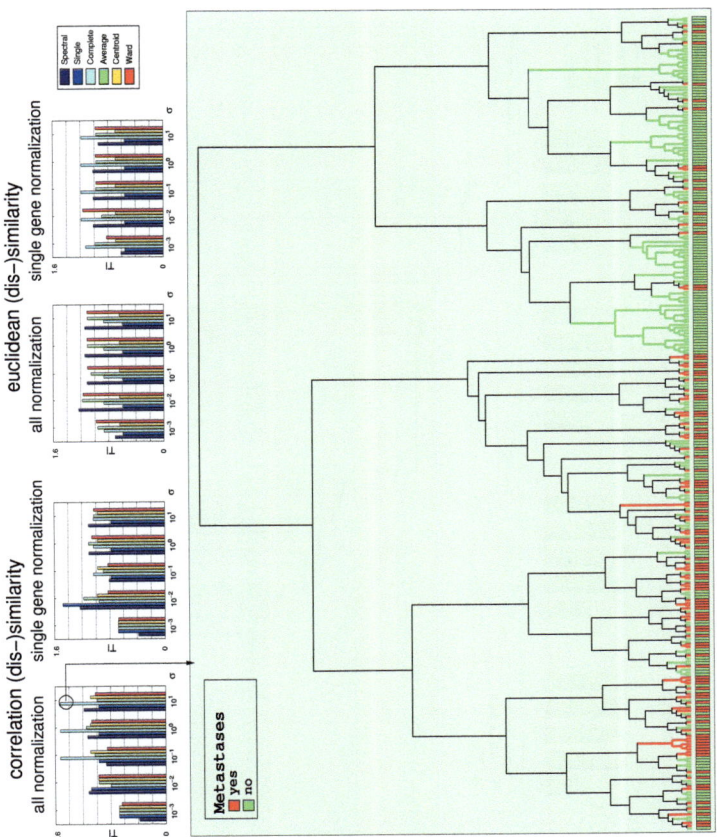

Figure 5.6: The van de Vijver data set is clustered by different cluster algorithms and parameterizations. The highest Tree Index is obtained for complete linkage clustering, the correlation dissimilarity measure, all normalization, and a scaling factor of 10. In the cluster tree, the subjects are colored according to their category (metastasis or no metastasis). It can be seen that in the very first split the data has been separated in an nearly homogeneous cluster (many subjects without metastasis) and a heterogeneous cluster. Such a split obtains a high splitting score and increases the Tree Index considerably.

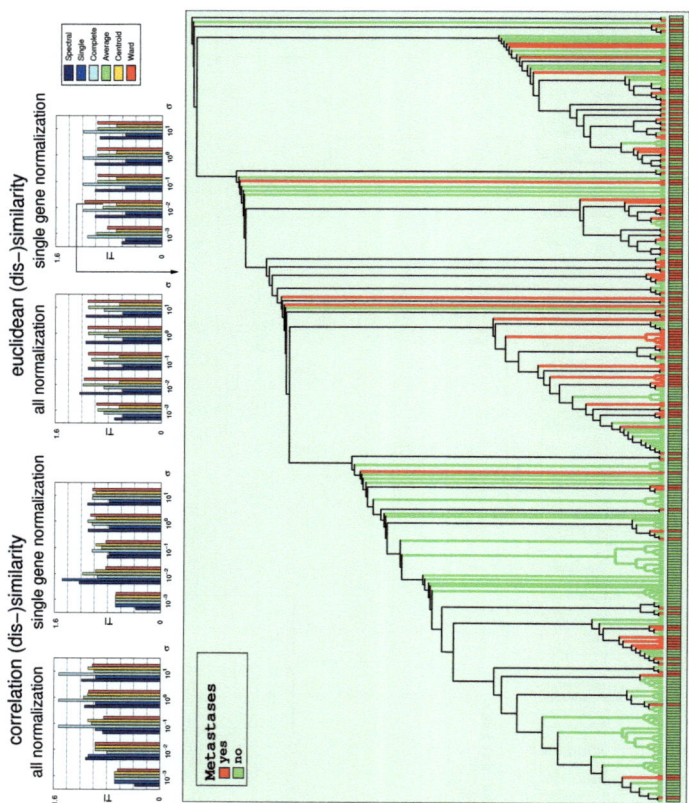

Figure 5.7: The tree indices obtained for the van Vijver data set are presented again, but a cluster tree of a mediocre quality is selected this time. It is obtained by average linkage clustering with the Euclidean dissimilarity measure, single gene normalization, and a scaling factor of 10^{-2}. In the cluster tree, the subjects are colored according to their category (metastases or no metastases). In contrast to Figure (5.6) the data is not that good separated according to its external label. In many splits only single elements are separated from the rest of the data. Consequently this leads to a less appealing visualization and a lower Tree Index.

5.3. THEORETICAL CONSIDERATIONS

n	tree structures (TS)	leaf orderings (LO)	ordered trees	fraction (TS/LO)
2	1	2	2	0.5
3	3	4	12	0.75
4	18	8	144	2.25
5	180	16	2880	11.25
6	2700	32	86400	83
8	$1.588 * 10^6$	128	$2.032 * 10^8$	12403
10	$2.572 * 10^9$	512	$1.317 * 10^{12}$	$5.023 * 10^7$
20	$5.645 * 10^{29}$	$5.243 * 10^5$	$2.960 * 10^{35}$	$1.077 * 10^{24}$
50	$3.286 * 10^{112}$	$5.629 * 10^{14}$	$1.850 * 10^{127}$	$5.838 * 10^{97}$
100	$1.374 * 10^{284}$	$6.338 * 10^{29}$	$8.710 * 10^{313}$	$2.168 * 10^{254}$
1000	$3.022 * 10^{4831}$	$5.358 * 10^{300}$	$1.619 * 10^{5132}$	$5.641 * 10^{4530}$

Table 5.1: The theoretical number of different tree structures, leaf orderings and ordered trees is computed for cluster trees of different sizes ($n = 2, \ldots, 1000$). Both the number of tree structures (TS) and the number of leaf orderings (LO) grow exponentially. However, TS is orders of magnitude higher than LO for large n as illustrated by the fraction TS vs. LO.

the data. Such splits obtain high splitting scores and are responsible for a high Tree Index.
In Figure (5.9) the tree indices for the Ramaswamy data set are presented again, but a cluster tree of a mediocre quality is selected this time. It can be seen that fewer homogenous cluster exist than in the main manuscript. The data is not that good separated according to its external label. In clusters of less than 20 elements it often occurs that only single elements are separated from the rest of data in the clusters. Consequently this leads to a less appealing image and a lower Tree Index.

5.3 Theoretical considerations

5.3.1 Tree structures and leaf orderings

The importance of identifying the algorithm and parameterization that yield objectively reasonable clustering results becomes obvious when calculating the number of possible different cluster trees (Figure 5.10). Theoretically, there are

$$\frac{1}{2^{n-1}}n!(n-1)! \tag{5.7}$$

different tree structures for a binary tree computed from n objects. Furthermore, there are 2^{n-1} different leaf orderings for each tree structure, resulting

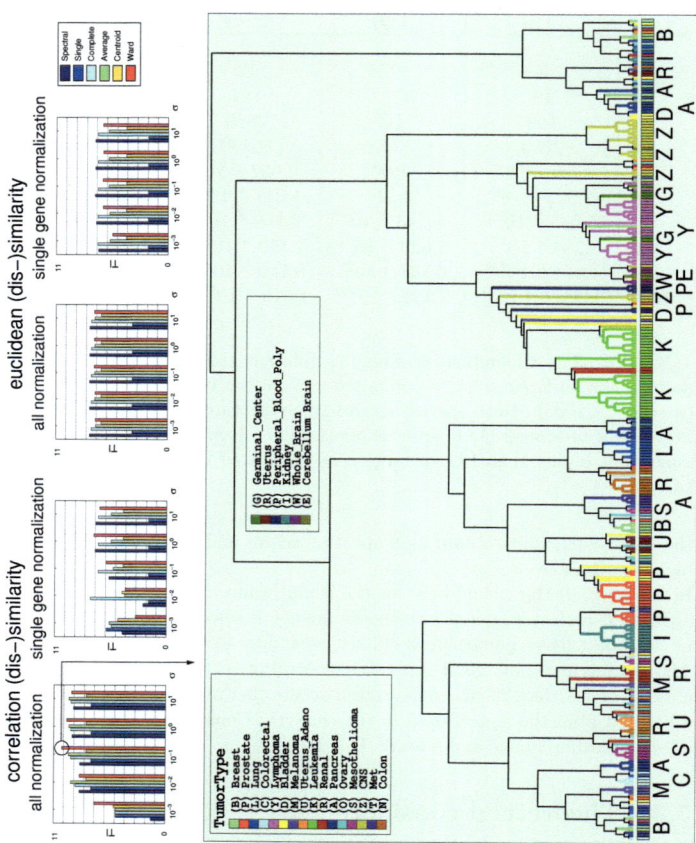

Figure 5.8: The Ramaswamy data set is clustered by different cluster algorithms and settings. The highest Tree Index is obtained for Ward clustering, the correlation dissimilarity measure, all normalization, and a scaling factor of 0.1. In the cluster tree, the subjects are colored according to their category (tumor type). Additionally, homogeneous clusters containing two or more elements are labeled with letters. It can be seen that in various splits, homogeneous clusters are separated from the rest of the data. Such splits obtain high splitting scores and are responsible for a high Tree Index.

5.3. THEORETICAL CONSIDERATIONS   65

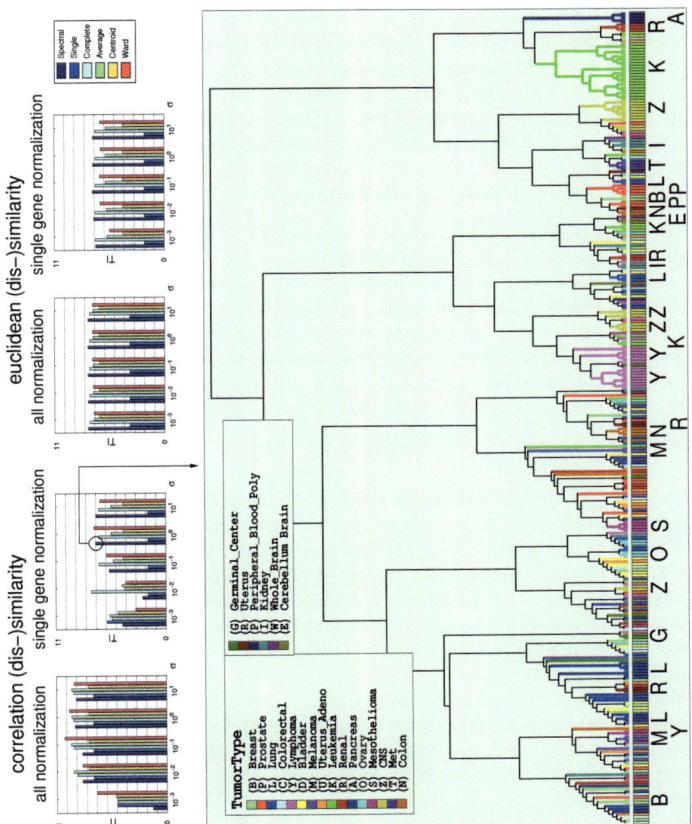

Figure 5.9: The tree indices for the Ramaswamy data set are presented again, but a cluster tree of a mediocre quality is selected this time. It is obtained by Spectral Clustering with the correlation similarity measure, single gene normalization, and a scaling factor of 10^0. In the cluster tree, the subjects are colored according to their category (tumor type). Additionally, homogenous clusters containing at least two elements are labeled with letters. In contrast to Figure (5.8) fewer homogenous cluster exist and the data is not that good separated according to its external label. In clusters of less than 20 elements it often occurs that only single elements are separated from the rest of data in the clusters. Consequently this leads to a less appealing visualization and a lower Tree Index.

in the theoretical number of $n!(n-1)!$ ordered trees. The Tree Index identifies the tree structure, but does not apply any leaf ordering. Numerous approaches for identifying the best leaf ordering have been proposed (Bar-Joseph et al., 2001; Ding, 2002). However, there are far more possible tree structures than leaf orderings (Table 5.1), which makes the identification of the best possible tree structure the more challenging task.

5.3.2 Different scoring methodologies

The TI is defined as the standard deviation of all splitting scores (equation 5.4 in section 5.1). Many splitting scores are zero (splits of homogeneous clusters) or close to zero (splits of small clusters), resulting in a mean score $\bar{S}$ close to zero. The number of splits R in a binary cluster tree, as obtained by hierarchical agglomerative clustering or spectral clustering, is given by $N-1$, whereas N is the number of clustered elements. Therefore, the result obtained by equation (5.4) is qualitatively similar to

$$\mathrm{TI}^p = ||\mathbf{S}|| = \left(\sum_{r=1}^{R} S_r^p \right)^{\frac{1}{p}} \qquad (5.8)$$

with $p = 2$. Using the l^p-norm allows to apply different scoring methodologies to define the final Tree Index: TI^1 is constant for all cluster trees obtained from the same data set. By increasing p, the impact of the high splitting scores is continuously increased. For $p = \infty$, the tree's quality is exclusively judged by the highest splitting score. $p = 2$ marks a preferable trade-off: All splitting scores are taken into account, whereas high splitting scores have a slightly higher impact on the final result compared to lower splitting scores.

More complex scoring methodologies might also take the tree level or the cluster size of each splitting score into account. However, a higher complexity also leads to a higher number of parameters that have to be adjusted and decreases the interpretability of the final index.

5.3.3 The probability of a split

When computing the probability of a split in Figure (5.2), we actually only compute the probability for the observed distributions in the clusters. The fact that the main cluster is separated in two classes, one with six and the other with four elements, is taken as a matter of course. Precisely, the probability for the observed partition and the observed distribution is given by:

$$p(\text{distribution}, \text{partition}) = p(\text{distribution}|\text{partition})p(\text{partition}) \qquad (5.9)$$

$p(\text{partition})$ is the probability for a cluster to split into l subclusters with m_i elements each. $p(\text{distribution}|\text{partition})$ is the conditional probability to

5.3. THEORETICAL CONSIDERATIONS

find the observed class distribution in the clusters and can be computed by equation (5.1) and (5.2).

For two subclusters ($l = 2$), the probability p(partition) to observe a partition with m_1 elements in the first cluster and $N - m_1$ elements in the second cluster is given by

$$p_{\text{partition}}(m_1; N) = \binom{N}{m_1} 2^{-N}. \tag{5.10}$$

$p_{\text{partition}}$ is independent of the number of classes k. For l subclusters, the probability p(partition) to observe a partition with m_i elements in the i-th cluster is given by

$$p_{\text{partition}}(m_i; N) = \frac{N!}{\prod_{i=1}^{l} m_i!} \, l^{-N}. \tag{5.11}$$

p(partition) becomes small if tiny clusters are separated from the rest of the data in a split. For this reason, a direct integration of p(partition) leads to desperate results in terms of degenerated trees and has been omitted for the computation of the TI. Nevertheless, an integration of p(partition) might be useful for outlier detection.

5.3.4 Cumulative hypergeometric distribution

For two categories ($\kappa = 2$) and two subclusters ($l = 2$), the cumulative hypergeometric distribution can easily be computed. Since $m_{11} + m_{12} = n_1$ and $m_1 + m_2 = N$, equation (5.1) can be rewritten as

$$p(m_{11}; N, n_1, m_1) = \frac{\binom{m_1}{m_{11}} \binom{N - m_1}{n_1 - m_{11}}}{\binom{N}{n_1}}. \tag{5.12}$$

$p(m_{11}; N, n_1, m_1)$ is the probability to observe m_{11} elements of category $\mathcal{C}_1$ in a cluster of size m_1, when there is a total of N elements, with n_1 elements of category $\mathcal{C}_1$. The cumulative hyperbolic distribution $p_c(m_{11}; N, n_1, m_1)$ is given by

$$p_c(m_{11}; N, n_1, m_1) = \sum_{x=0}^{m_{11}} \frac{\binom{m_1}{x} \binom{N - m_1}{n_1 - x}}{\binom{N}{n_1}}. \tag{5.13}$$

and computes the probability that there are m_{11} elements or less (!) of category $\mathcal{C}_1$ in a cluster of size m_1. In Figure (5.11) both the hypergeometric distribution and the cumulative hypergeometric distribution are displayed. Figure (5.11a) plots the probability to observe $m_{11} \in [0, 100]$ of category $\mathcal{C}_1$ elements in a cluster of size $m_1 = 100$, when there is a total of $N = 500$ elements, with $n_1 = 200$ elements of category $\mathcal{C}_1$. The blue area describes the probability to observe at least m_{11} (here: $m_{11} = 35$) elements of category $\mathcal{C}_1$. This probability can directly be expressed by the cumulative hypergeometric distribution (Figure 5.11b).

For the general case (κ categories and l subclusters), a generalized form of the cumulative polyhypergeometric distribution has to be computed. Such a computation is a challenging task and is also computationally expensive.

5.4 Discussion

Hierarchical cluster algorithms are frequently used in exploratory data analysis as it is often performed for microarray data. Different cluster algorithms and parameterizations produce different clustering results. The algorithm and parameterization leading to the most appealing cluster visualization need to be detected according to a specific external label. An appealing cluster tree is characterized by splits dividing a heterogeneous cluster into nearly homogeneous subclusters regarding externally given additional variables which are interpreted as labels. In this chapter, a novel index, the Tree Index was proposed. It is based on the probability of each single split in a cluster tree. The Tree Index can identify the cluster algorithm and parameterization yielding the clustering best suited for visualization. The direct analysis of the structure of the cluster tree has the advantage that — in contrast to cluster indices that work on partitions — there is no need to estimate the number of clusters or to cut the cluster tree at some level.

In the experiments performed in this chapter, the applied cluster algorithms, preprocessings and (dis-)similarity measures were varied to create a large range of possible tree visualizations. Since the application of hierarchical agglomerative clustering and spectral clustering as well as the computation of the Tree Index are not very time-consuming and can be performed automatically for a large range of parameterizations, many more preprocessings and (dis-)similarity measures could be tested. Other important issues like gene selection or outlier deletion might also be considered to obtain cluster trees with even higher tree indices.

5.4.1 Outlook

The Tree Index optimizes the tree structure of the cluster tree, not its display. The leaf ordering inside the cluster tree is still arbitrary. For a binary tree with n leaves, there are 2^{n-1} possible visualization (section 5.3.1). Even though this is far less than the number of possible tree structures, it is recommended to apply a leaf ordering algorithm (Bar-Joseph et al., 2001; Ding,

5.4. DISCUSSION

2002) for the final visualization. Finally, enhanced visualization techniques with carefully selected graphical attributes (line width, color scale, etc.) should also be considered.

The Tree Index returns a positive value for any cluster tree and label, but it is not normalized. It is also biased towards the number of categories. Usually the Tree Index increases with the number of categories, since statistically it becomes less likely to separate a homogeneous cluster from the rest of the data, if there are more categories. However, in practice, it often happens that distinctive homogeneous groups are separated from the rest of the data. The Tree Index achieves its maximum (upper bound) if complete homogeneous clusters are obtained in the first split (if there are two categories) or in the very first splits (if there are more than two categories). The Tree Index achieves its minimum (lower bound) for a complete random cluster tree and random label. In chapter 6, the upper and lower bound are used to derive a normalized Tree Index (NTI) which is 0 for a complete random cluster tree and random label and 1 for a sharp clustering.

The upper bound of the Tree Index can be statistically derived, whereas a computation of the lower bound is not straight forward and more theoretical work for a proper modeling of cluster tree distributions has to be done. Nevertheless the lower bound can be approximated using Monte Carlo simulations as described in section 4.3.

The Tree Index can also be used to assess the robustness of cluster trees. To which extent does the cluster tree change, if noise is added to some components of the data? This application is especially interesting for microarray data, since for every gene and subject, the variance of gene expression can be estimated from replicata spots. However, there are only very few papers that incorporate the gene expression variance in their analysis (Tjaden, 2006). Also, the influence of the scaling parameter of the (dis-) similarity measure have to be further examined. Interestingly the cluster trees remain robust for a large range of values until suddenly large branches change instantly.

In this chapter, the Tree Index was applied on cluster trees obtained from clustered biological samples. The Tree Index might also be applied to trees clustering genes, which requires the incorporation of further biological knowledge. A possible external label is the primary function of a gene. Many databases exist for gene annotation and gene ontology (Mewes et al., 2002; GO-Consortium, 2000). However, a gene is usually involved in more than only one function or pathway and the gene annotations are still incomplete. Adaptations of the Tree Index are necessary to apply it with such multi-variate and incomplete external labels.

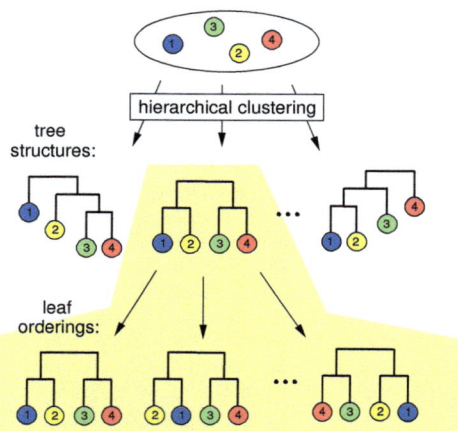

Figure 5.10: For $n = 4$ objects, there are 18 different tree structures for a binary tree. For each of these tree structures, there are eight different leaf orderings, resulting in a total number of 144 different ordered binary trees.

5.4. DISCUSSION

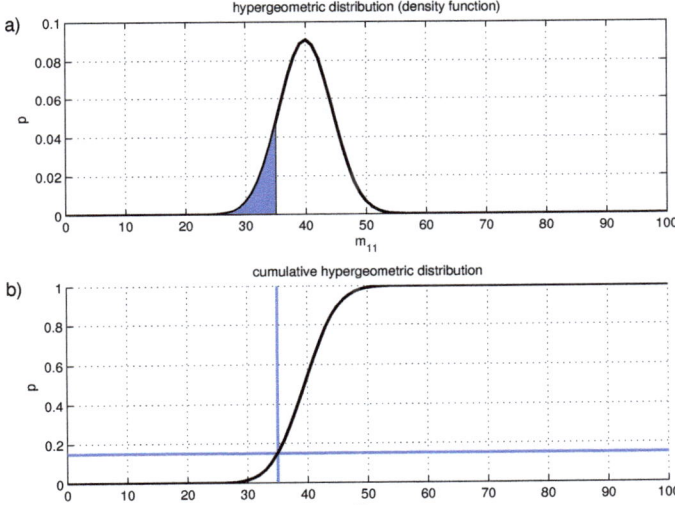

Figure 5.11: Both the hypergeometric distribution (a) and the cumulative hypergeometric distribution (b) are displayed. In (a) the probability to observe $m_{11} \in [0, 100]$ elements of category $\mathcal{C}_1$ in a cluster of size $m_1 = 100$ is plotted, when there is a total of $N = 500$ elements, with $n_1 = 200$ elements of category $\mathcal{C}_1$. The blue area describes the probability to observe at least m_{11} (here: $m_{11} = 35$) elements of category $\mathcal{C}_1$. This probability can directly be expressed by the cumulative hypergeometric distribution function (b).

Chapter 6

A Normalized Tree Index to identify correlated clinical parameters

Hierarchical agglomerative clustering is the basis for most visual data mining tasks in microarray applications (previous chapter). Compared to non-hierarchical cluster algorithms, it has the advantages that the number of clusters does not have to be specified in advance. This property is of utmost importance since the number of clusters is usually unknown making a precise a priori prediction of the number of clusters impossible. A second reason for the frequent application of hierarchical agglomerative clustering is its visualization ability. The intrinsic hierarchical cluster structure of the data becomes visually accessible at once in the computed cluster tree. It is common practice to visualize the computed cluster tree in combination with the clustered microarray data (the primary data) and additional information (the secondary data) that is available for the clustered samples (Figure 3.3).

Microarray technology is currently entering the field of medicine. Medical studies are often characterized by a high amount of clinical parameters (secondary data). Many new insights into the mechanisms of diseases can be obtained when the microarray data is analyzed in combination with the clinical which consists of master data, vital data, laboratory data and outcomes (with respect to diseases of interest) that is available for each subject. Clinical data can be considered as a set of observations on the phenotypic level. There are observations on the molecular level (e.g. protein expression), macroscopic observations (e.g. skin color, tumor size, outcome) as well as behavioral observations (e.g. nutrition, alcohol, sport). One issue in which the researcher is often interested in is the identification of clinical parameters that are correlated with the microarray data. A high correlation between a clinical parameter and the microarray data indicates that there might be a common underlying mechanism or pathway. The detection of a correlation provides fundamental insights, since it links the clinical parameter, the phenotype, to the genotype represented by the microarray data. The identification of a high correlation between a phenotype and the genotype helps to formulate new hypothesis and to obtain new insights into the complex mechanisms of diseases and life itself.

The visual inspection of cluster trees allows to estimate the correlation between the clustered microarray data and clinical parameters. However, this approach becomes infeasible for studies with large numbers of samples and many clinical parameters. Furthermore, the number of clinical parameters that is available for each subject is supposed to increase in the next decade, since an increasing number of hospitals stores all kinds of clinical data in hospital information systems. Medical departments also become more and more cross-linked. Therefore, an automated computation of the correlation between clinical parameters and microarray data is needed to identify correlated clinical parameters.

One way to compute the correlation between a clinical parameter (variable) and the microarray data is to compute the correlation between the clinical parameter (first variable) and every single gene (second variable) and to combine the results in a final correlation coefficient. Depending on the type of variables, statistics provides various methods to compute the correlation between two variables. For interval data, Pearson's correlation coefficient r (Fisher, 1915) computes the correlation between two variables whereas each variable is normalized to zero mean and unit variance beforehand. For ordinal data, the correlation between two variables can be computed by Spearman's rank correlation coefficient ρ (Sachs, 2002), which is a robust measure which can even be applied on small sample sizes. The only requirement is that the original data of any two successive ranks has to be approximately equidistant. In cases where this can not be assumed, Kendall's τ (Kendall, 1938) has to be applied. For nominal data, the chi-square test, Pearson's contingency coefficient, or the corrected contingency coefficient measure the correlation between any two variables (Sachs, 2002).

A major drawback of the different correlation and contingency coefficients is that they can only be used to compute the correlation between a clinical parameter and a single gene. The information contained in microarray data is usually not contained in single genes, but in so-called metagenes (Huang et al., 2003). Thus, a direct computation of the correlation between single genes and clinical parameters in order to identify correlated clinical parameters does not capture the major trend of information that is hidden in the data. Microarray data rather has to be considered in its entirety, and an analysis always has to be done in a holistic way.

In this chapter a novel index, the Normalized Tree Index (NTI), is developed to compute a correlation coefficient between nominal clinical parameters and microarray data. The NTI is an extension to the Tree Index (TI) introduced

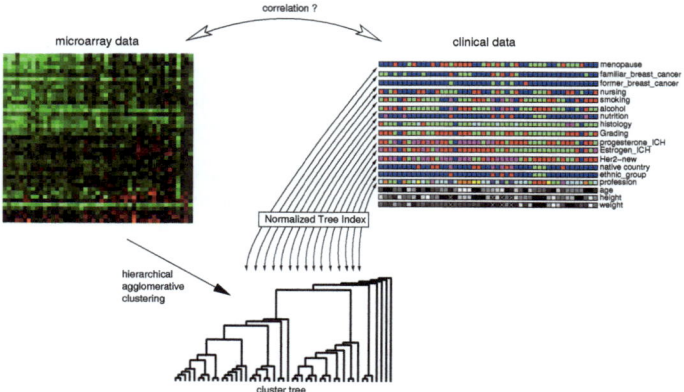

Figure 6.1: The Normalized Tree Index (NTI) is used to compute a correlation coefficient between nominal clinical parameters and microarray data. In a first step, the microarray data is clustered by hierarchical agglomerative clustering using standard settings. In a second step, the computed cluster tree is evaluated using the NTI. For each nominal clinical variable that is available, a NTI is computed that measures the correlation between that variable and the clustered microarray data. This permits to identify clinical parameters that are highly correlated with the microarray data, while analyzing the microarray in its entirety.

in the previous chapter. It is zero for a complete random clustering and random label and one for a sharp clustering. Furthermore, an empirical p-value is derived which measures the level of significance of the detected correlations between external labels and clustered microarray data. In a first step, the microarray data is clustered by hierarchical agglomerative clustering using standard settings (Figure 6.1). Thereby, the complete microarray data is taken into account. In a second step, the computed cluster tree is evaluated using the NTI. For each nominal clinical variable that is available, a NTI is computed measuring the correlation between that variable and the clustered microarray data. By this approach the microarray data is considered in its entirety and clinical parameters that are correlated with the microarray data can be identified.

The NTI is applied on two breast cancer data sets to compute correlations between the microarray data and clinical data.

6.1 Methods

In the precious chapter, the TI is used to identify the algorithm and parameterization yielding the clustering that is best suited for visualization. As noticed in section 5.4, the TI has the drawback that it is biased with respect to the number of classes of the external label. If the number of categories increases, the TI also increases. In chapter 5, this drawback is of no importance since the TI is used with a constant external label and thus a constant number of classes. In order to apply the TI in combination with variable external labels, an extension to the TI, the Normalized Tree Index (NTI), is developed in this section. The NTI computes a correlation coefficient between nominal parameters and hierarchically clustered data. Furthermore, a p-value is derived that measures the level of significance of the detected correlation between external labels and clustered data.

6.1.1 The Normalized Tree Index (NTI)

The Normalized Tree Index (NTI) is an extension to the TI and computes a correlation coefficient between nominal parameters and hierarchically clustered data. A normalization is applied to the TI in such a way that the NTI is zero for a complete random clustering and one for a clustering in which the clustered elements are grouped in complete concordance with the external label. The normalization is obtained by making use of the minimal TI (TI_{min}) and the maximal TI (TI_{max}) that can be obtained by the given external labels. The values TI_{min} and TI_{max} are computed empirically using a Monte Carlo simulation (section 4.3 and Figure 6.2). Figure (6.2a) shows the clustering that is obtained when applying hierarchical agglomerative clustering to the data. In Figure (6.2b) $r = 10000$ random clusterings with randomly permuted labels (based on the given external label) are generated. The clustering with the lowest TI is an empirical estimation for TI_{min}. In Figure (6.2c) $s = 10000$ sharp clusterings for the provided external label are generated. The cluster tree with the highest TI is an empirical estimation for TI_{max}. With the estimations for TI_{min} and TI_{max}, the NTI is defined by

$$NTI = \frac{TI - TI_{min}}{TI_{max} - TI_{min}} \quad (6.1)$$

6.1.2 p-value

Natural fluctuation in the data might lead to constellations in which the clustered data seems to be correlated with external labels, but in fact the correlation has occurred by chance. The computation of a p-value allows to detect such false identifications of correlations. Let H_0 be the null hypothesis that there is no correlation between the microarray data and a clinical parameter. A p-value lower than a significance level of 5%, 1%, or 0.1%

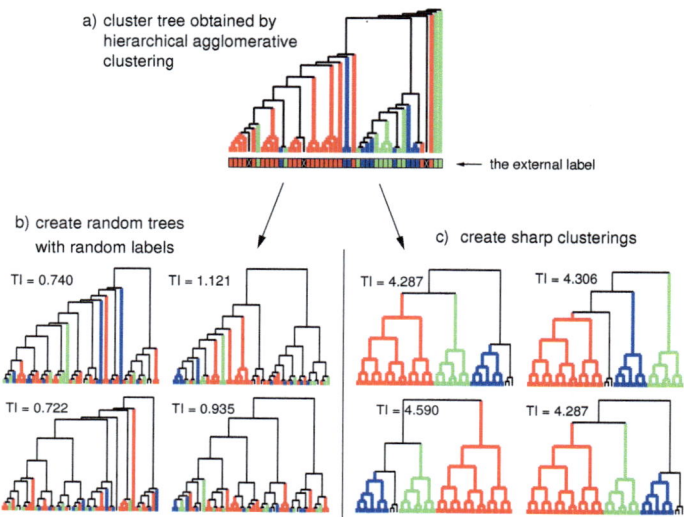

Figure 6.2: The clustering that is obtained when applying hierarchical agglomerative clustering to the data is shown in (**a**). The branches and leaves of the cluster tree are painted according to the given external class label. Missing values are visualized by black leaves. In (**b**) $r \geq 10000$ random clusterings with randomly permuted labels (based on the given external label) are generated. The clustering with the lowest TI is an empirical estimation for TI_{min}. In (**c**) $s \geq 10000$ sharp clusterings for the provided external label are generated. The cluster tree with the highest TI is an empirical estimation for TI_{max}.

means a rejection of H_0. The p-value can either be derived theoretically or empirically. In this chapter, a Monte Carlo simulation is used to compute an empirical p-value for the TI and NTI. Since the p-value is not altered by a normalization of the TI, it is equal for the TI and the NTI. For simplicity, the computation of the p-value is derived for the TI in the following.

Let t be the TI of the tree obtained by a hierarchical cluster algorithm (e.g. hierarchical agglomerative clustering). The empirical p-value is defined by the fraction of TIs obtained from random trees and randomly permuted labels that is equal or higher than t (Figure 6.3):

$$p = \int_{u \geq t}^{\infty} du \qquad (6.2)$$

6.1. METHODS

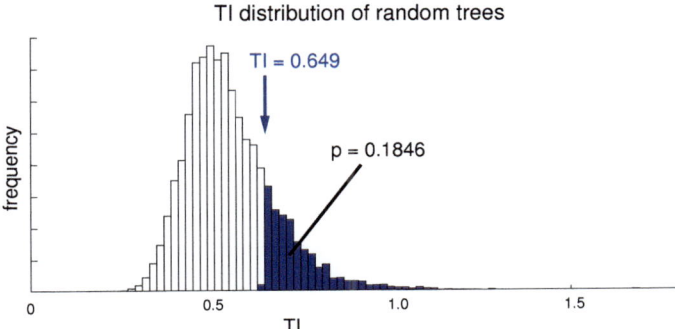

Figure 6.3: An empirical p-value for the TI (as well as for the NTI) is obtained using a Monte Carlo simulation: A TI is computed $r \geq 1000$ times for random trees and randomly permuted labels. The p-value is defined by the fraction of TIs that is equal or higher than the TI of a non-random cluster tree (here: 18.46%). The resulting p-value of $0.1846 > 0.05$ indicates that there is no significant correlation between the clustered data and the label.

For practical use, p can be approximated by

$$p \approx \frac{1}{r} \sum_{\substack{i=1 \\ t_i > t}}^{r} 1 \qquad (6.3)$$

with t_i being the TI of the i-th random tree and i-th randomly permuted label. A $p \geq 0.05$ means that H_0 (no correlation) cannot be rejected. A $p < 0.05$ (0.01, 0.001) means that the rejection of H_0 is statistically significant at the 5% (1%, 0.1%) level. The number r of computed random trees and randomly permuted label has to be sufficiently large to obtain a statistical significant rejection of H_0 at the 5% (1%, 0.1%) level. $r \geq 1000$ random trees are required to theoretically achieve a statistical significant rejection of H_0 at the 0.1% level.

Example Let us assume that hierarchical agglomerative clustering of some data leads to a TI of $t = 0.688$ (Figure 6.3). Let us further assume that the Monte Carlo simulation reveals that 18.46% of TIs obtained from random clusterings and randomly permuted labels are higher than t. The resulting p-value of 0.1846 indicates that H_0 (no correlation) cannot be rejected at the 5% level of significance.

clinical parameter	num	categories		
metastasis	2	(1) no	(2) yes	
positive lymph nodes	2	(1) no	(2) yes	
event death	2	(1) no	(2) yes	
estrogen receptor	2	(1) negative	(2) positive	
National Institute Health criteria	2	(1) 0	(2) 1	
St.Gallen consensus criteria	2	(1) 0	(2) 1	
conservative flag	3	(1) 0	(2) 1	(3) 2

Table 6.1: The clinical parameters and their categorizations in the van de Vijver breast cancer data set.

6.2 Results

The NTI and p-value is applied on two microarray data sets. The first data set is the breast cancer data set of van de Vijver et al. (2002), which is described in section 5.2. In addition to the microarray data, six nominal clinical parameters are available for each subject (Table 6.1). The second data set is a preliminary data set taken from the yet unpublished Bielefeld breast cancer project led by Anika Tauchen[1] and Anke Becker[2]. A selected set of 212 marker genes is analyzed for 87 samples taken from 49 patients. One main contribution of the project, in contrast to other microarray breast cancer studies, is the high amount of clinical parameters that has been collected for each of the patients. As summarized in Table (6.2, left column) and Table (6.3, left column), 29 clinical parameters are selected for correlation analysis. Some of these parameters are interval parameters. To apply the NTI, they have to be converted to nominal parameters by parameter-specific transformations (e.g. the values of the parameter *age* are divided into the six categories <40, 40 to 49, 50 to 59, 60 to 69, 70 to 79, and >80.). Moreover, when reasonable, the categories of some nominal variable are merged (e.g. the categories of the parameter *progesterone receptor IHC* are transformed to the categories *negative* (for values 0 to 1), *intermediate* (for values 2 to 8) and *high positive* (for values 9 to 12)). All specific transformations are listed in Table (6.2, right column) and Table (6.3, right column).

Both data sets are preprocessed and clustered as follows: The logarithms of ratios are scaled to $[-1, 1]$ (all normalization). Then they are clustered by hierarchical agglomerative clustering using average linkage and a distance metric (dissimilarity measure) based on the correlation between a pair of subjects. This correlation distance metric $d_{ij} \in [0, 1]$ of two expression

---

[1] Fakultät für Gesundheitswissenschaften, University of Bielefeld, Germany
[2] Zentrum für Biosystemanalyse, University of Freiburg, Germany

6.2. RESULTS

clinical parameter	num	categories
age	6	(1) <40 (2) 40 to 49 (3) 50 to 59
		(4) 60 to 69 (5) 70 to 79 (6) > 79
sample type	3	(1) biopsie before chemotherapy
		(2) biopsie after chemotherapy
		(3) operation (after chemotherapy)
BMI	3	(1) normal (18.5 to 25)
		(2) overweight (25 to 30) (3) obese (>30)
native country	6	(1) Germany (2) Poland (3) Russia
		(4) Taiwan (5) Sri Lanka (6) Turkey
ethnic group	2	(1) Europe (2) Asia
nursing	2	(1) no (2) yes
nursing period	4	(1) none (2) short (1 to 5 months)
		(3) intermediate (6 to 14 months)
		(4) long (>14 months)
menopause	2	(1) no (2) yes
smoking	5	(1) always non-smoker (2) sometimes
		(3) regular (4) often (5) again non-smoker
alcohol	5	(1) never (2) no longer
		(3) less than once a month
		(4) 1 to 3 times a week (5) daily
sport	3	(1) nothing (0h/week) (2) little (1 to 4h/week)
		(3) plenty (>5h/week)
sleep	3	(1) little (<7h/day) (2) normal (7-9h/day)
		(3) plenty (>9h/day)
familiar breast cancer	2	(1) no (2) yes
histology	4	(1) ductal (2) lobar (3) not definable
		(4) mucous ductal
T (tumor dimension)	5	(1) T0 (2) T1 (3) T2 (4) T3 (5) T4
N (lymph nodes)	3	(1) N0 (2) N1 (3) N2
Grading	2	(1) G2 (2) G3
Progesterone	3	(1) negative (0 to 1) (2) intermediate (2 to 8)
receptor IHC		(3) high positive (9 to 12)
Estrogen	3	(1) negative (0 to 1) (2) intermediate (2 to 8)
receptor IHC		(3) high positive (9 to 12)
Her2-new	3	(1) negative (2) intermediate (3) positive
intended operation	5	(1) ablatio and axilla (2) ablatio and sentinel
		(3) BET and sentinel (4) ablatio (5) BET

Table 6.2: The clinical parameters 1 to 21 and their categorizations for each subject in the Bielefeld breast cancer data set are listed. Interval parameters are converted to nominal parameters by the indicated transformations in parentheses.

clinical parameter	num	categories
inspection	4	(1) noconspicuity
		(2) inflammatory mamma-carcinoma
		(3) plateau phenomenon (4) other
lateral acoustical shadow	2	(1) no (2) yes
dorsal acoustic attenuation	2	(1) no (2) yes
axilla	2	(1) unsuspicious (2) suspicious
tumor size (mammogramm)	3	(1) small (0 to 9mm)
		(2) intermediate (10 to 25mm)
		(3) large (>26mm)
micro lime	2	(1) no (2) yes
chemoregime	5	(1) TAC (2) ACDoc (3) Geparquattro
		(4) FEC (5) Geparquinto
herceptin treatment	2	(1) no (2) yes

Table 6.3: The clinical parameters 22 to 29 and their categorizations for each subject in the Bielefeld breast cancer data set are listed. Interval parameters are converted to nominal parameters by the indicated transformations in parentheses.

profiles $\mathbf{x}_i$ and $\mathbf{x}_j$ of dimension g is defined as

$$d_{ij} = \frac{1}{2} - \frac{\sum_{k=1}^{g} \mathbf{x}_{ik}\mathbf{x}_{jk}}{2g} \qquad (6.4)$$

By applying the NTI on cluster trees obtained from real-world data sets, we simulate the scenario where a biomedical researcher is looking for clinical parameters that are correlated with the microarray data.

A NTI and p-value is computed for each clinical parameter listed in Tables 6.1 to (6.3). A summary of all results is shown in Figure (6.4). For both data sets, the highest NTI is obtained for the estrogen receptor. The number of stars indicates the level of significance of the correlation. One star means that the rejection of H_0 (no correlation) is statistically significant at the 5% level. Two stars mean that the rejection of H_0 is statistically significant at the 1% level. Three stars mean that the rejection of H_0 is statistically significant at the 0.1% level. No stars mean that H_0 cannot be rejected.

In the upper part of Figure (6.4), the results for the van de Vijver breast cancer data set are shown. The highest NTI is obtained for the clinical parameter *estrogen receptor (ESR1)*. The correlation between the clinical parameters *metastasis, event death,* and *estrogen receptor (ESR1)* and the microarray data is statistically significant at the 0.1% level. The *StGallen consensus criteria* is statistically significant at the 1% level. In the lower part of Figure (6.4), the results for the Bielefeld breast cancer project are shown.

6.3. DISCUSSION   81

The highest NTI is obtained for *estrogen receptor IHC*. The correlations between *BMI, native country, progesterone receptor IHC* and *estrogen receptor IHC* and the microarray data are statistically significant at the 0.1% level. The correlations of the parameters *age, T (tumor dimension) grading* and *intended operation* are statistically significant at the 1% level. The correlations of the parameters *ethnic group, nursing period, menopause, N (lymph nodes), Her2-new, inspection, tumor size (mammogramm)* and *chemoregime* are statistically significant at the 5% level.

Cluster trees for the parameters *metastasis, event death, positive lymph nodes* and *estrogen receptor (ESR1)* of the van de Vijver data set are displayed in Figure (6.5) and (6.6). Clustering results for the parameters *estrogen receptor IHC, progesterone receptor IHC, T (tumor dimension), grading, native country* and *BMI* of the Bielefeld data set are displayed in Figures (6.7) to (6.9).

6.3 Discussion

In this chapter a novel index, the Normalized Tree Index (NTI), is developed to compute a correlation coefficient between nominal clinical parameters and microarray data. The NTI is an extension to the TI as described in the previous chapter. It is zero for a complete random clustering and random label and one for a sharp clustering. Furthermore, an empirical p-value is derived which measures the level of significance of the detected correlations between external labels and clustered data. A high correlation between a clinical parameter and the microarray data indicates that there might be a common underlying mechanism or pathway. This linkage between the phenotype (the clinical parameter) and the genotype (the microarray data) helps to formulate new hypothesis and aids to obtain new insights into the complex mechanisms of diseases and even life itself.

Another benefit that arises from the detection of highly correlated clinical parameters is the following: Clinical parameters that are highly correlated with a set of genes have the ability to make the analysis of genes containing redundant information dispensable. The removal of these genes with redundant information helps to identify sets of core marker genes.

Even though applied to microarray data in a medical setting, the NTI can be applied to any complex data that fulfills some basic requirements: First, it should be possible to cluster the primary data by some hierarchical cluster algorithm (e.g. hierarchical agglomerative clustering, spectral clustering (section 2.2)). Second, some supplementary data (secondary data) should be available for each clustered item.

The NTI computes a correlation coefficient between nominal clinical parameters and the microarray data. Ordinal and interval parameters have to be converted to nominal parameters by parameter-specific transformations (Table 6.2 and 6.3). Such transformations always imply a loss of information. However, a reduction of the data of an ordinal or interval parameter to a few biological relevant categories can also help to avoid overfitting. In Table 6.2, the interval-scaled clinical parameters *progesterone receptor IHC* and *estrogen receptor IHC* have been transformed to nominal parameters with three categories of negative (0 to 1), intermediate (2 to 8) and high positive (9 to 12) values. Nevertheless, strategies for a direct application of the NTI on ordinal and interval data need to be developed.

Hierarchical agglomerative clusters and a computation of the NTI are advantageous compared to the following method that is sometimes used to obtain a correlation coefficient: A classifier is trained on the microarray data. A selected parameter is used to rate the correlation depending of the ability of a classifier to predict the correct label in a leave-one-out setting. The higher the classification rate, the higher the correlation between microarray data and clinical parameter. The major drawback of this approach is that a visualization is not provided this way. A high classification rate indicates a high correlation, but there is no way to retrace how the specific classification rate has been obtained. Homogeneous clusters, outliers, and other interesting patterns cannot be identified this way.

6.3. DISCUSSION

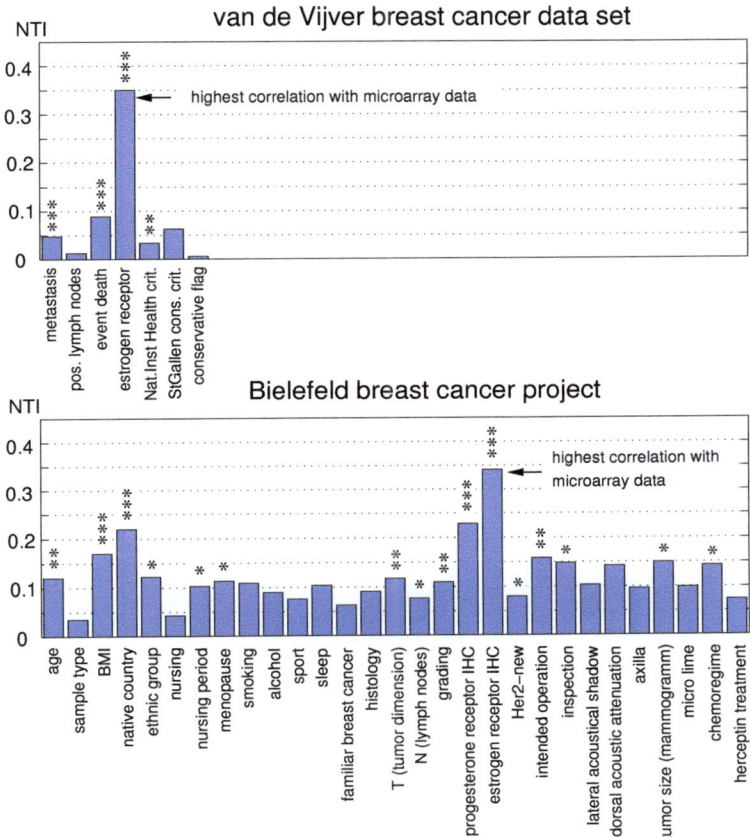

Figure 6.4: A NTI and p-value is computed for each available clinical parameter. For both data sets, the highest NTI is obtained for the estrogen receptor. The number of stars indicates the level of significance of the correlation. One star means that the rejection of H_0 (no correlation) is statistically significant at the 5% level. Two stars mean that the rejection of H_0 is statistically significant at the 1% level. Three stars mean that the rejection of H_0 is statistically significant at the 0.1% level. No stars mean that H_0 cannot be rejected.

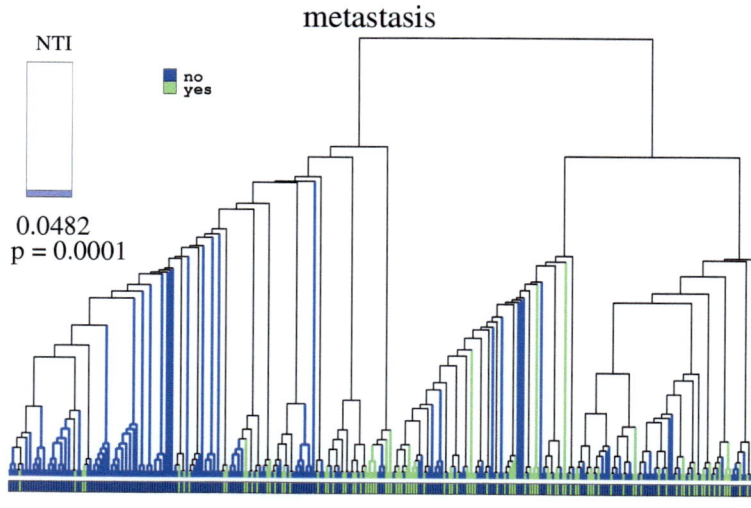

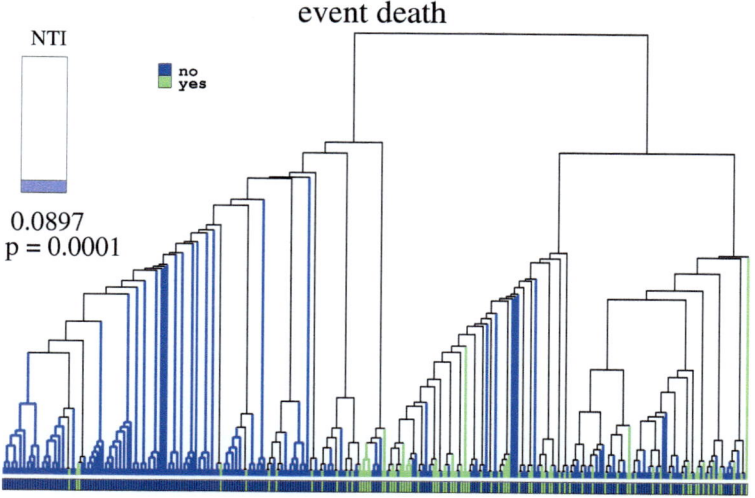

Figure 6.5: The cluster tree obtained from the van Vijver data set is painted and evaluated with respect to the clinical parameters *metastasis* and *event death*. The p-values < 0.001 reveal that the rejection of H_0 (no correlation) is statistically significant at the 0.1% level. According to the NTI, *event death* is more correlated to the microarray data than *metastasis*.

6.3. DISCUSSION

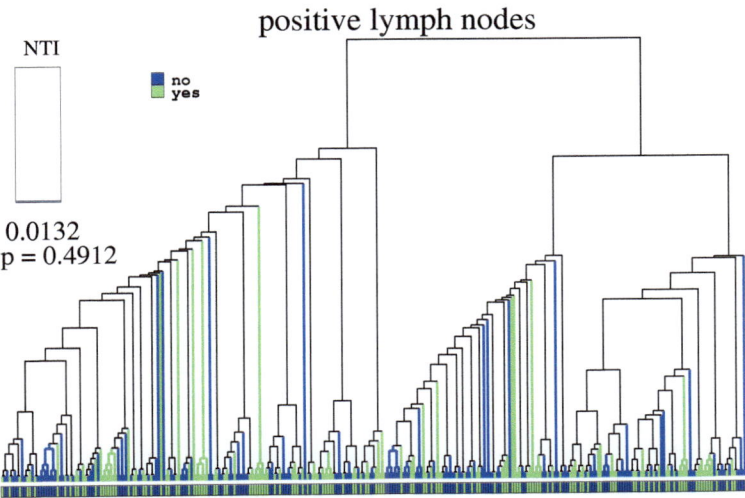

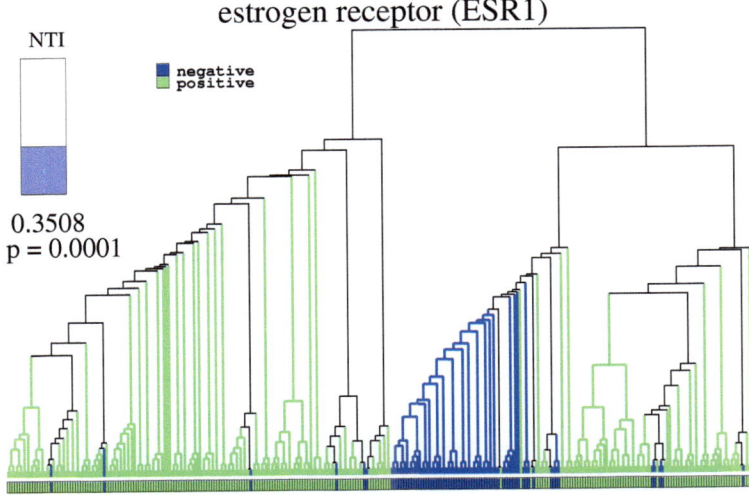

Figure 6.6: The cluster tree obtained from the van Vijver data set is painted and evaluated with respect to the clinical parameters *positive lymph nodes* and *estrogen receptor (ESR1)*. The p-value of 0.4912 indicates that there is no correlation between *positive lymph nodes* and the microarray data. In contrast to that, there seems to be a very high correlation between *estrogen receptor (ESR1)* and the microarray data, since the rejection of H_0 is statistically significant at the 0.1% level.

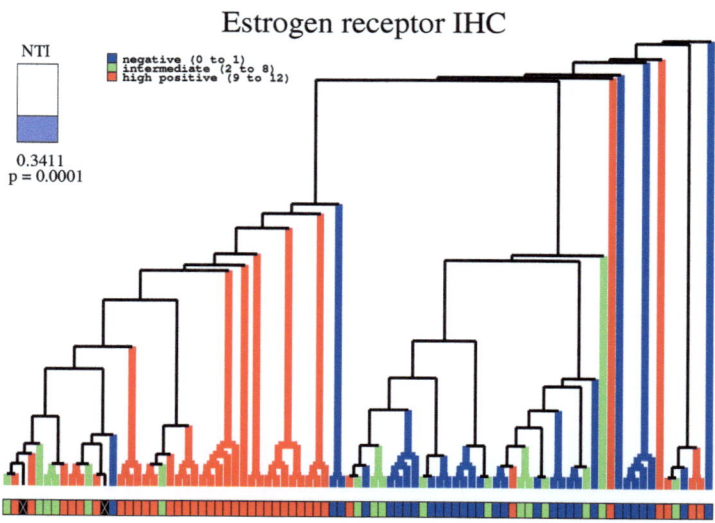

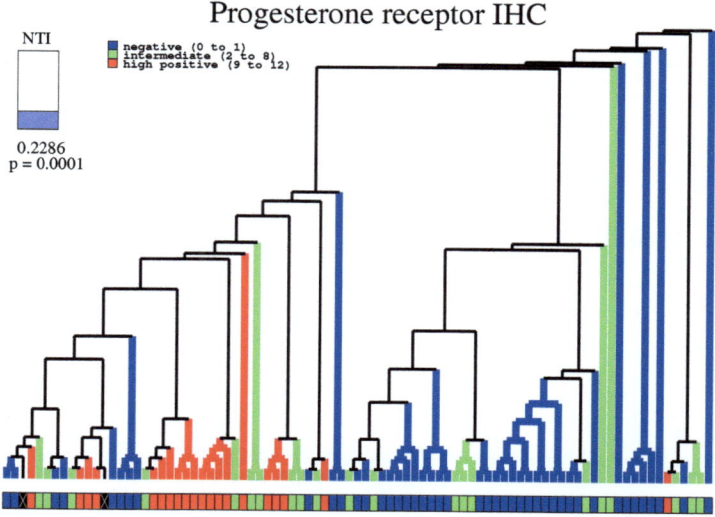

Figure 6.7: The cluster tree obtained from the Bielefeld data set is painted and evaluated with respect to the clinical parameters *estrogen receptor IHC* and *progesterone receptor IHC*. These are the two parameters with the highest NTI in the Bielefeld data set. The p-value indicates that there is a correlation at the 0.1% significance level for both parameters.

6.3. DISCUSSION

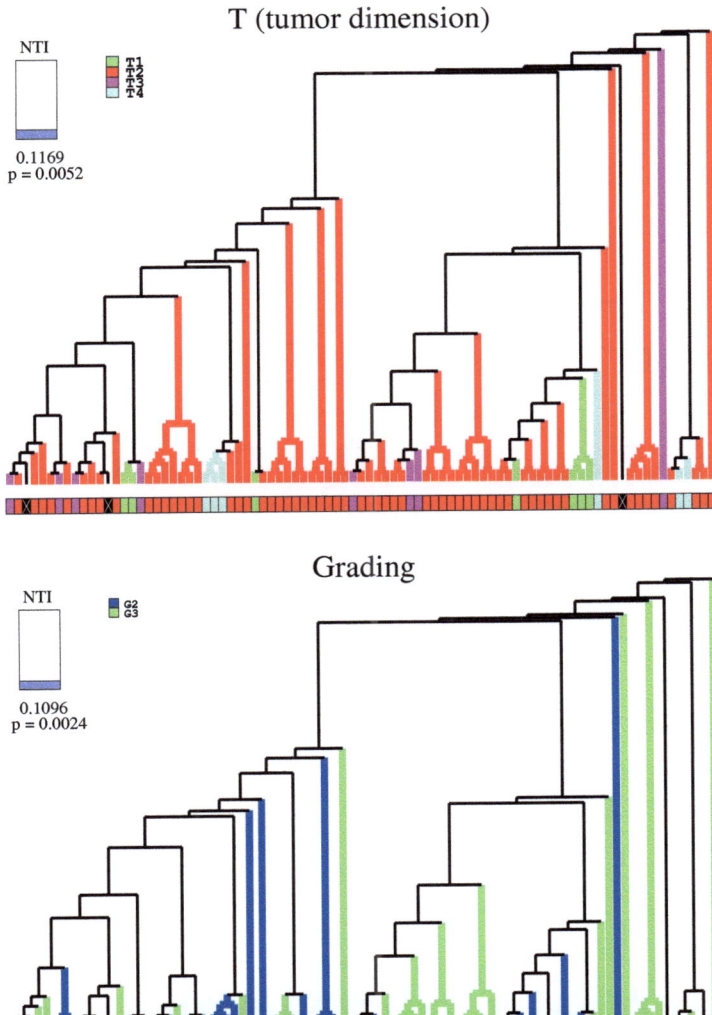

Figure 6.8: The cluster tree obtained from the Bielefeld data set is painted and evaluated with respect to the clinical parameters T *(tumor dimension)* and *grading*. For both parameters, a correlation at the 1% significance level is reported. The NTI of ≈ 0.1 indicates that there is a slight correlation between these clinical parameters and the microarray data.

88   CHAPTER 6. NORMALIZED TREE INDEX

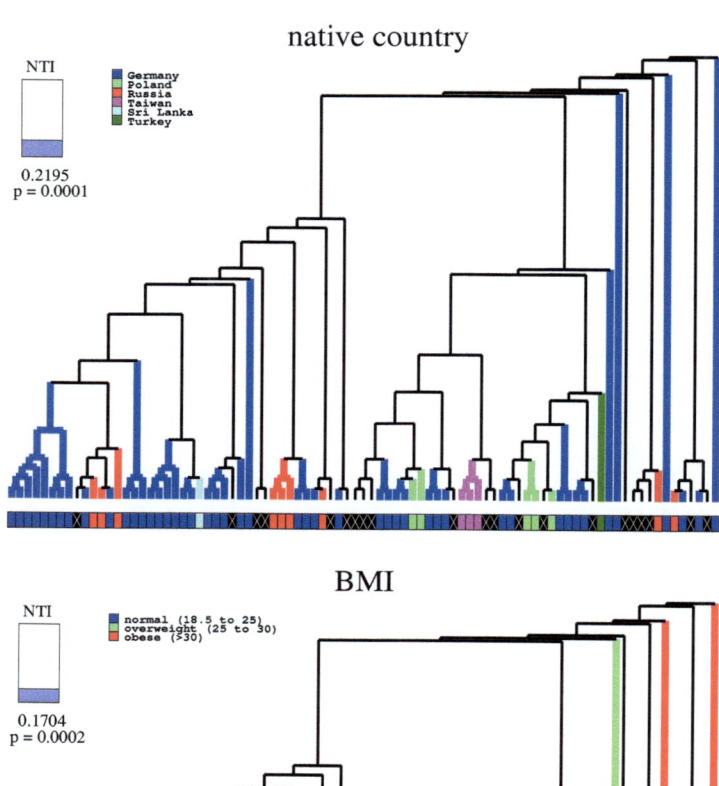

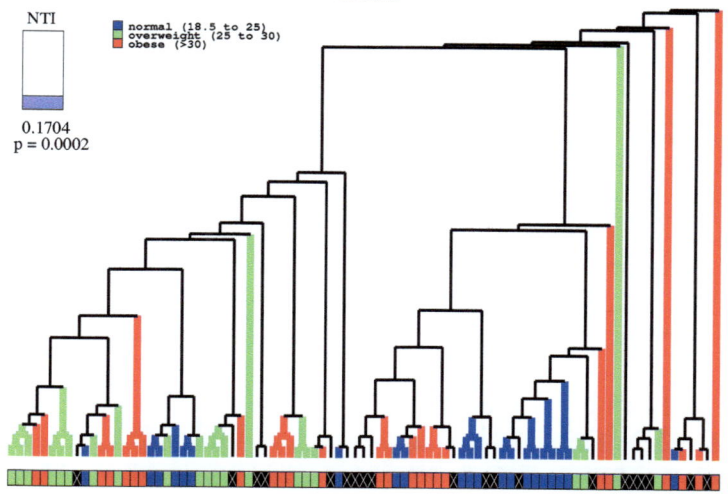

Figure 6.9: The cluster tree obtained from the Bielefeld data set is painted and evaluated with respect to the clinical parameters *native country* and *BMI*. Both parameters are correlated with the microarray data at the 1% significance level.

Chapter 7

Fusing biomedical multi-modal data for exploratory data analysis

In modern biomedical research data from different sources, multi-modal data or complex data, is often linked together for an holistic analysis. Especially in clinical studies concerning cancer research, clinical and categorical data is completed by gene expression data from microarray experiments in the last decade (Quackenbush, 2001; Ochs, 2003). The clinical data contains age, weight and sex of the patient, the size or the grade of the tumor, information about the lymph nodes, or results from a histological analysis (van't Veer et al., 2002) and many other parameters. Categorical data denotes the most important parameter for the respective study. Depending on the type of study, this parameter can be the tumor malignancy, the patients survival time or the success of a chemotherapy.

In the last years, the number of experiments and studies using microarray technology has increased considerably. Especially for breast cancer research there are at least 39 studies, and for about two third of them data is available on the internet (Brennan, 2005). Up to 25,000 genes can be analyzed simultaneously, even though often only a fraction of these genes is selected and used for further analysis (Dettling and Buehlmann, 2004). The major challenge is how all this clinical, categorical and genomic data can be analyzed in an integrative manner. This problem is further increased by the high dimensionality of the data. Usually the number of available experiments (number of samples) is approximately of the same magnitude or even smaller than the number of genes (dimensionality of data space) analyzed, which makes the application of statistical test methods impracticable. Many machine learning methods can handle such difficulties, but most of them are based on pairwise similarities, which cannot be defined appropriately for multi-modal data. Considering all these aspects makes a more interactive, exploratory data analysis seem more reasonable. To allow an exploratory study, the multi-modal data, which is usually distributed in several media (tables, flat files) must be integrated into one representation, combining visualizations of all kinds of available data. A simultaneous visual inspection of all modalities enables the detection of patterns and structure in the data when browsing through and zooming into the image.

In this chapter, an integrative multi-modal visualization approach based on the Self-Organizing Map (SOM) (Kohonen, 1990) is proposed. The basic idea is to render a multi-modal visualization to display multi-modal data. A visualization is designed that consists of dimension reduction and multivariate object display, i.e. data glyphs. The SOM algorithm comprises the aspects dimension reduction, clustering and visualization and is well suited for the analysis and visualization of the microarray data (Tamayo et al., 1999; Wang and et al., 2002).

Thus the first data modality, the microarray data is fed into the SOM. Displaying the trained SOM with the U-matrix approach (Ultsch, 1993a) visualizes structural features of the high dimensional microarray data space. The visualized U-matrix is expanded by introducing multivariate data glyphs in order to display clinical and categorical data.

Using a metaphoric display approach (Nattkemper, 2005) the SOMs U-matrix is rendered as an underwater sea bed with color and texture. In contrast to the REEFSOM presented in Nattkemper (2005) the underwater landscape can then be completed with glyphs generated from data from different sources, which was not used for training of the SOM. In this chapter, a kind of metaphoric glyph is used, a so called fish glyph. The fish glyphs have two groups of parameters that describe shape or colors in order to display clinical data by shape and categorical features with color. The resulting images are both informative and entertaining and can easily be interpreted by the biomedical collaborator, since specific knowledge about the SOM algorithm is not required. Its visual inspection might reveal interesting structural patterns in microarray, clinical and categorical data.

7.1 SOM-based sea bed rendering

The Self-Organizing Map (Kohonen, 1989) provides an unsupervised learning algorithm for dimension reduction, clustering and visualization which is easy to implement (Kohonen, 2001). To visualize the trained SOM, several approaches have been proposed: The feature density of the trained SOM prototype vectors is displayed based on smoothed histograms (Vesanto, 1999), the U-matrix (Ultsch, 1993a), or by clustering the prototype vectors (Vesanto and Alhoneimi, 2000; Wu and Chow, 2004). For the special case of very large SOMs, fish eye view or fractal view have been proposed (Yang et al., 1999). In addition, the SOM visualization can be augmented by text

7.2. THE FISH GLYPH

labels, as for instance the WEBSOM (Honkela et al., 1997) or a single feature analysis with a component plane view (Kaski et al., 1998). Also automatic feature selection has been proposed to render icons for displaying the SOM prototype vectors on a grid (Rauber and Merkl, 2001).

The U-matrix as proposed by Ultsch (1993a) is probably the most applied visualization framework for SOM, especially for SOM with a large number of neurons. The U-matrix visualizes the data structure by a display of approximated data densities at the SOM grid nodes. For each node, the average distance to all its neighboring nodes is computed. These average distances are displayed by a height profile or by a colored plane. In this chapter, both techniques are combined to visualize the U-matrix as a colored height profile. For visualization of the underwater scenario, the U-matrix is visualized the other way round, i.e. the *depths* of the sea bed are drawn proportional to the average distances. So in the display clusters of very different data are separated by valleys. However, it should be noticed that in the case of overlapped and interconnected clusters as they often occur when analyzing microarray data, the U-matrix approach might show some limitations.

7.2 The fish glyph

Glyphs (or icons) are parameterized geometrical models that are used for an integrated display of multivariate data items. The idea is to map the variables of one data item to the parameters of one glyph so that the visual appearance of the glyph encodes the data variables.

Glyph approaches can be classified as being *abstract* or *metaphoric*. Abstract glyphs are basic geometric models without direct symbolic or semantic interpretation like profiles (du Toit et al., 1986), stars (Siegel et al., 1972), boxes (Hartigan, 1975a). To display more variables or also data relations, abstract glyphs can get quite complex like the customized glyphs (Ribarsky et al., 1994; Kraus and Ertl, 2001), shapes (Shaw et al., 1999) or infochrystals (Spoerri, 1993). Such glyphs can be powerful tools for a compact display of a large number of variables and relations. However, the user must spend considerable time for training to be able to use these tools effectively.

Since the idea of using metaphoric display is quite natural, metaphoric glyphs have been proposed in the earliest years of information visualization already. In 1970, the well known Chernoff faces (Chernoff, 1971) were introduced for multivariate data display. The idea of rendering data faces may get new stimuli from advances in computer graphics and animation (Noh and Neumann, 1998) since a large range of algorithms exist to render faces in different emotional states. However, the successful application of Chernoff faces seems to be restricted to data with a one-dimensional substructure, like social and economic parameters as in Dorling (1994), Alexa and Müller

92   CHAPTER 7. FUSING BIOMEDICAL MULTI-MODAL DATA

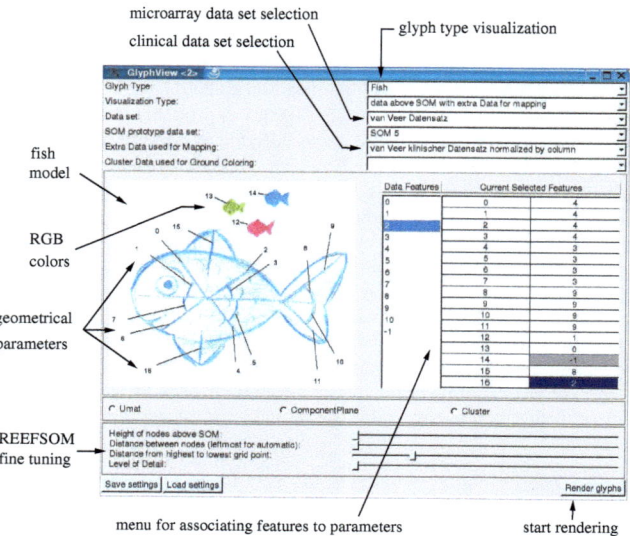

Figure 7.1: The fish glyph GUI: In the left half a fish cartoon shows the geometrical parameters p_k of the fish glyph. This is used for associating the clinical variables and categories to the parameters $x_j^{(i)}$. Parameters $p_0, \ldots, p_{11}, p_{15}$ and p_{16} encode the geometrical properties of the fish and can be used to display different clinical variables. Parameters p_{12} to p_{14} encode the RGB color of the fish and can be used to display a category. The right side is used to map clinical variables and categories to the 17 fish glyph parameters. A value of -1 encodes, that no variable is associated to this parameter. In this case a default value is taken. In the lower part of the GUI, fine tuning can be applied, parameter settings can be stored and loaded and the rendering process of the REEFSOM can be triggered.

(1998) and Smith et al. (2002). Similar approaches use stick figures (Pickett and Grinstein, 1988), a parameterized tree (Kleiner and Hartigan, 1981) or wheels (Chua and Eick, 1998). To visualize the SOM in a metaphoric manner, the designs of the U-matrix landscape and the data glyphs need to be synchronized. To this end a fish shaped glyph is developed. The fish glyph is used to display (i) the prototypes of the SOM or (ii) all the items of the data set or (iii) both. In mode (ii) and (iii) the data set items are to be visualized on top of the sea bed, i.e. the SOM. But, the computation of an appropriate two dimensional grid position for each data item on the SOM

7.2. THE FISH GLYPH

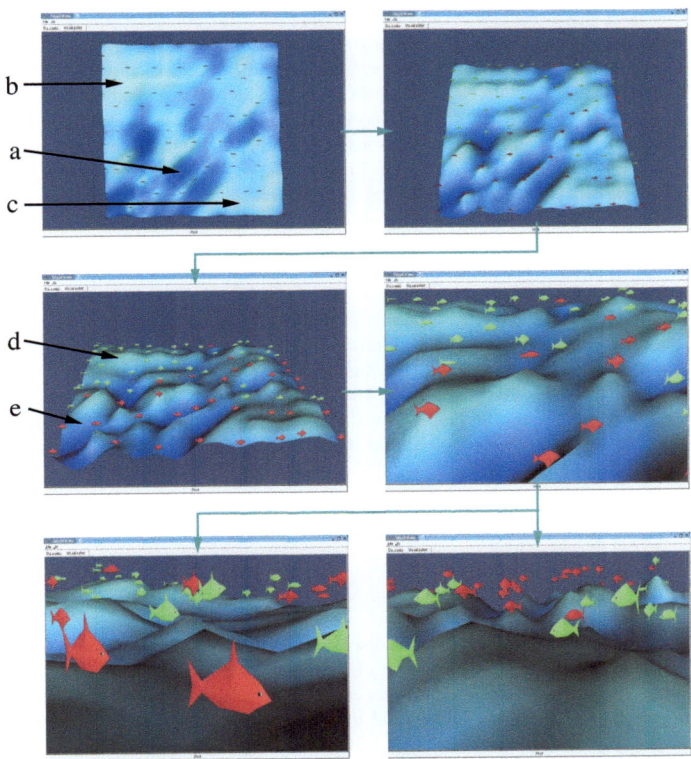

Figure 7.2: A flight into the REEFSOM of the microarray data set is shown. The sea bed is barely divided by one abyss (**a**) into two plateaus (**b** and **c**). An inspection of the fish glyphs reveals, that the top left plateau is dominated by green fish corresponding to patients who survived the next five years (**d**). The front is dominated by red fish (patients who died within the next five years) which are placed in the abyss as well as on the plateau (**e**).

(relative to the SOM node coordinates) is a nontrivial problem. The most naive approach is to take the grid coordinates of the winner node This approach must fail, if the number of data items per winner node exceeds one, since in this case two fish must be rendered at the same position. A more advanced solution is to interpolate the two dimensional position from the grid node positions of several nodes. In the literature, some approaches have been proposed, most of them applying advanced interpolation algorithms. In our first version of the software, an exact positioning of the data items on the SOM is disclaimed. Each data item is rendered at a random position in the close vicinity of its winner node. On first sight, this strategy looks a bit crude, but it is motivated by several arguments. First, several solutions to the interpolation problem have been proposed and there is not *one* solution which is accepted by the entire community. Second, one important feature of each data item is its cluster prototype, i.e. its nearest neighbor. If the interpolation leads to suboptimal results, the data item, or its glyph, is rendered at a position closer to another node, which makes it visually infeasible to identify the winner node correctly. Third, the random strategy is the computationally least expensive one.

The fish model consists of two kinds of parameters, 14 geometric parameters (six angles and eight arc lengths) and three color values (RGB). The mapping of the clinical values to the fish parameters can either be done automatically or can be defined by the user using the fish glyph GUI (Figure 7.1). Prior knowledge can be used to map similar clinical values to related fish parameters.

In Figure (7.2) a flight into the REEFSOM illustrates, how the color and shape of fish, rendered on top of a U-matrix sea bed, varies.

7.3 Application

To illustrate the application and usefulness of the REEFSOM for the exploratory analysis of biomedical multi-modal data, results are shown for the van't Veer breast cancer data set (van't Veer et al., 2002). It consists of microarray, clinical and categorical data and is available via internet. The microarray data comprises the analysis of 25000 genes for 78 primary breast samples. For each gene and sample the logarithm of basis 10 of the intensity and the ratio ($[-2, 2]$) are provided. The original gene pool was reduced (mainly by using statistical methods) in three steps to 5000, 230 and finally 70 genes forming sets of marker genes that are somehow related with breast cancer outcome (van't Veer et al., 2002). Since gene selection usually helps to improve the results in the domain of microarray data, it is focused on the gene set with 70 genes to compute the REEFSOM in this chapter. More sophisticated gene selection techniques might further improve the REEFSOM results but are not considered here. The clinical data contain the age of the subject (28 to 62 years), the grade (I to III) and diameter (2 to 55 mm) of the tumor, the oestrogen (0 to 100) and progesterone receptor status (0 to 100), angioinvasion (yes or no), metastasis (yes or no) and lymphocytic infiltrate (yes or no). A subset of these variables is used to render the shape of the fish glyphs. The categorical data consists in the subjects survival during

7.3. APPLICATION

Table 7.1: The mapping of the clinical and categorical features to the parameters of the fish glyph

type	feature	visual.	parameter	fish glyph parameter
clinical	grade	shape	$x_0 \ldots x_3$	top
clinical	diameter	shape	$x_4 \ldots x_7$	bottom
clinical	age	shape	$x_8 \ldots x_{11}$	tail (caudal) fin
clinical	lymphocytic infiltrate	shape	x_{15}	top (dorsal) fin
clinical	angioinvasion	shape	x_{16}	lower (pectoral) fin
category	survival $\leq$ 5 years	color	x_{12}	red
category	survival $>$ 5 years	color	x_{13}	green

the following five years (yes or no). This information is used to define the color of the fish.

7.3.1 Mapping

In Table (7.1) the mapping of the clinical and categorical features to the parameters of the fish glyph is summarized. In order to enhance the contrast between different fish glyphs the software allows to map a feature to more than one parameter of the fish glyph. Here this is done for the clinical features grade, diameter and age which are mapped to four parameters (two lengths and two arcs) each. Figure (7.3) shows four visualizations of fish glyphs and illustrates the significance of their shape and color.

7.3.2 Results

The SOM is trained with one million training steps whereas a linear decreasing neighborhood and learning rate are used. Preliminary experiments with SOMs of sizes between 5×5 and 100×100 trained on the microarray data set with 70 genes revealed the best results for a SOM of size 15×15 using visual inspection. The SOM result could probably be further improved by fine-tuning of the parameters and by using objective measures for the map organization and topology preservation Venna and Kaski (2005). Fish glyphs are integrated to represent the clinical and categorical data. The clinical data is used to render the shape of the fish and the categorical data specifies the color of the fish. A flight into the computed REEFSOM is shown in Figure (7.2). In Figure (7.4) results from an exploratory data analysis are described.

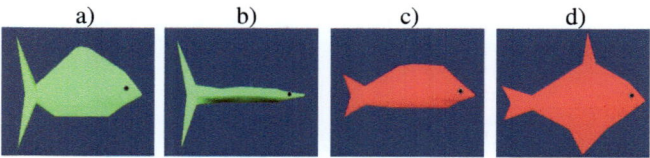

Figure 7.3: Fish **(a)** represents a subject with a high age (large tail fin), who survived the following five years (green color). There is no lymphocytic infiltrate (no top fin) and no angioinvasion (no lower fin). The tumor has grade III (huge top) and has a medium diameter (medium bottom). Fish **(b)** represents a subject with a high age (large tail fin), who survived the following five years (green color). There is no lymphocytic infiltrate (no top fin) and no angioinvasion (no lower fin). The tumor has grade I (small top) and has a tiny diameter (tiny bottom). Fish **(c)** represents a subject with a low age (small tail fin), who died within the following five years (red color). There is no lymphocytic infiltrate (no top fin) and no angioinvasion (no lower fin). The tumor has grade II (medium sized top) and has a small diameter (small bottom). Fish **(d)** represents a subject with a low age (small tail fin), who died within the following five years (red color). There is a lymphocytic infiltrate (top fin) and angioinvasion (lower fin). The tumor has grade III (large top) and has a large diameter (large bottom).

7.4 Summary and Discussion

The REEFSOM (Nattkemper, 2005), a metaphoric display, is applied and further improved such that it allows the simultaneous display of biomedical multi-modal data for an exploratory analysis. Visualizations of microarray, clinical, and category data are combined in one informative and entertaining image. The U-matrix of the SOM trained on microarray data is visualized as an underwater sea bed using color and texture. The clinical data and category data are integrated in the form of fish shaped glyphs. The color represents a category (the main information one is interested in) and the shape is modified according to selected clinical features.

In order to compare the REEFSOM with other data analysis approaches a test scenario is imaginable where test persons are asked to detect structures and patterns in either artificial or real-life data sets.

The REEFSOM has the fundamental advantage that it is multi-modal itself, and thus expecially well suited for the display of multi-modal data. The *geology modus* (U-matrix displayed as sea bed) is combined with a *fauna modus* (fish glyphs) or *fauna modi* (fish shape representing the clinical data and fish color representing the category). The user can direct his attention

7.4. SUMMARY AND DISCUSSION

to the modus of his choice or to both. Additional modi allow the integration of further data sources, e.g a *flora modus* might be introduced for displaying features of biomedical images (X-ray, CT, MRI).

Advances in this chapter reveal that the REEFSOM is well suited for the exploratory data analysis of multi-modal data since its ability to combine visualizations of microarray, clinical and category data. The resulting images are intuitive, entertaining and can easily be interpreted by the biomedical collaborator, since specific knowledge about the SOM algorithm is not required. Visual inspection enables the detection of interesting structural patterns in the multi-modal data when browsing through and zooming into the image.

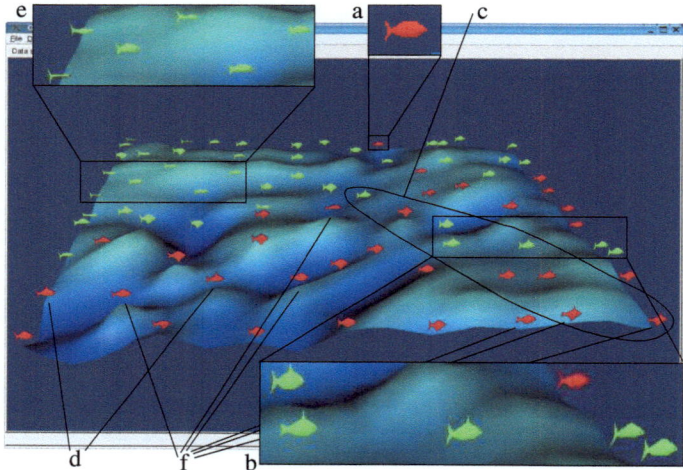

Figure 7.4: Subjects who survived the following five years (green fish) are separated from those who died within the following five years (red fish), except a few outliers (**a** and **b**). The single red outlier (**a**) is placed in a region dominated by green fish indicating that its gene expression profile is similar to those subjects who survived the following five years. Also its clinical features do not indicate any deviation from the surrounding green fish. The group of outliers (**b**) consists of five fish. All of them have tumor grade III (huge top) and three of them have lymphocytic infiltrate (top fin). Interestingly subjects with lymphocytic infiltrate (top fin) cluster together (**c**) except two outliers (**d**). This indicates that the gene expression profile of subjects with lymphocytic infiltrate are similar. The upper left half is dominated by subjects who survived the following five years. Many of them have a tumor of grade I or II (small or middle size top with a small tumor diameter (small bottom) (**e**). In contrast to that most of the subjects in the front have tumor grade III (huge top). Many subjects who died within the following five 5 years (red fish) are still young (small tail fin) (**f**).

Chapter 8

Taxonomic classification of short DNA fragments

The emerging field of metagenomics allows, for the very first time, to study the collective genomes (metagenomes) of microbes in free-living microbial communities (Handelsmann et al., 2007). The simultaneous study of the large number of species on a genomic level demands for new algorithmic approaches to process the high amount of sequenced DNA fragments.

One major task is to assign a DNA fragment to its originating species. Such a classification would be a crucial step in the analysis of an environment on an organismal level, leading to a more complex way of describing and comparing environmental states. Another metagenomic challenge results from the observation that many species have not yet been sequenced, leaving us with a narrow sample as reference. To obtain contigs from metagenomic data, a binning of the sequence reads is helpful for assembly. This binning task is addressed by classifying sequence reads to predefined categories at a specific phylogenetic rank. The most challenging task is to classify them at species rank, but a classification at higher phylogenetic ranks is also helpful. Genus, Order, Class, Phylum, and Superkingdom represent the most commonly used taxonomic ranks (Figure 8.1 and 3.5).

In order to estimate phylogenetic differences between certain species of interest, two approaches have been developed:

The traditional approach is based on sequence similarity (homology) taking into account only part of the genome (i.e. a single gene or a marker gene). The major drawback for the detection of marker genes is the need for sequence alignment, a technique for which many pitfalls can be encountered (Li, 1997), sampling of representative sequences, lateral gene transfer, or recombination are among the most common. Other attempts to estimate phylogenetic distance involve the use of ribosomal RNA molecules, gene content, gene order, protein domain content, etc. Moreover, multiple sequence alignments are computationally very expensive.

Chapter 8. Taxonomic Classification of DNA Fragments

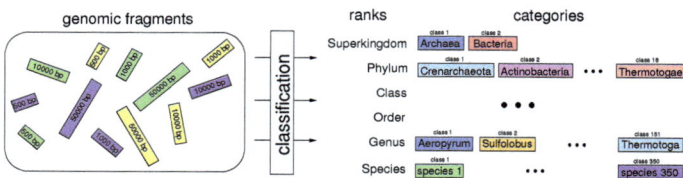

Figure 8.1: One major task in metagenomics is to classify DNA fragments of varying lengths at different phylogenetic ranks. The most challenging task is to classify them at species rank, but a classification at higher phylogenetic rank is also helpful. Genus, Order, Class, Phylum, and Superkingdom represent the most commonly used taxonomic ranks.

The second approach is alignment-free and is based on nucleotide composition (Teeling et al., 2004; Abe et al., 2006; McHardy et al., 2007). The information is directly computed from the nucleotide sequence of genomes or non-assembled fragments disregarding prior identification of functional regions are taken into account (Gupta, 1998; Stuart et al., 2002; Qi et al., 2004; Chapus et al., 2005). Such methods have the potential to classify even short genomic sequences and help in the evaluation of trends in microbial diversity, novel genes, and genome evolution. A powerful characteristic that enables to capture evolutionary relationships between species and permits a classification of DNA fragments is the genomic signature which is defined as a set of short oligonucleotide patterns in a sequence (Karlin and Burge, 1995). Genomic signatures are species-specific and can be computed from complete genomes, but also from variable-length DNA fragments in any part of the genome (Deschavanne et al., 1999). A genomic signature can be regarded as a feature vector that can be processed by any data mining or machine learning algorithm. McHardy et al. (2007) applies the concept of genomic signature to train a Support Vector Machine (SVM) on fragments of 100 Kb in order to classify fragments of ≥ 1 Kb of 340 species at the taxonomic ranks Domain, Phylum, Class, Order, and Genus) with high accuracy.

The classifier that performs the task of classifying sequence reads to support binning at a specific phylogenetic rank should cover the following three aspects: First, it should be accurate in classification. Second, it should be scalable to process the large data sets that are present in metagenomics. Third, it should enable a data visualization to provide means for inspection and for feature space exploration, a feature that is usually not provided by sophisticated classifiers in the machine learning or data mining domain. Most black box classifiers such as SVMs do only address the first and sometimes the second of these requirements.

To cover all aspects of accurate classification, scalability, and data visualization, feature vectors representing genomic fragments are processed by a special variant of Kohonen's Self-Organizing Map (SOM) (Kohonen, 1990), the H^{2}SOM (section 2.3.1). In genomic studies, the standard SOM has already been applied very successfully to classify environmental DNA fragments with length of 10 Kbp or more (Abe et al., 2002, 2005, 2006, 2007). The standard SOM projects the data to a two-dimensional flat Euclidean space, a space that might not correspond to the intrinsic structure of genomic data. It is more likely that genomic sequences are structured hierarchically in the same way as their corresponding species are grouped into kinships relations as represented in the tree of life. Hierarchically organized data grows exponentially and thus requires a mapping into a geometric space with corresponding behavior. To this end, the hyperbolic SOM (HSOM) applies a tree-like grid in hyperbolic space. It has already been successfully applied in text mining (Ontrup and Ritter, 2006) and first successes have also been reported for the embedding of high-dimensional feature vectors representing genomic sequences (Martin et al., 2007). A special ultra-fast hierarchical training scheme is applied in the hierarchical-growing hyperbolic SOM (H^{2}SOM), which enables to deal with the exponentially growing amount of data in metagenomic studies.

In order to further decrease the required minimum length of DNA fragments for a proper classification, three different representations (feature vectors) of genomic sequences and DNA fragments based on the genomic signature are evaluated: In a first experiment, frequencies of oligonucleotide patterns are directly taken as features, and are combined to a feature vector for each complete genome or DNA fragment. In a second approach, features are developed that take the general importance of each oligonucleotide pattern into account. These features are similar to the *term frequency - inverse document frequency (tf-idf)* features, successfully applied in text mining (Salton et al., 1975). In a third approach, features containing the enhanced contrast between over- and underrepresented patterns are evaluated.

In this chapter, genomic sequences of 350 prokaryotic organisms (section 3.2.5) are used. This represents a vast majority of sequenced organisms from the two domains archaea and bacteria. DNA fragments of 0.2 - 50 Kbp are classified to the most commonly used taxonomic categories at the ranks Superkingdom, Phylum, Class, Order, Genus, and Species. Thereby, the classification of DNA fragments sequenced by the Sanger technology or 454 pyrosequencing as well as assembled contigs is addressed. Feature vectors obtained from complete genomic sequences or DNA fragments are used to train a H^{2}SOM. Subsequently the trained model is used as classifier (section 2.3.2) to classify DNA fragments of shorter lengths. It is shown that a phylogenetic classification of DNA fragments of 0.2 - 50 Kbp is possible with a high accuracy in a H^{2}SOM framework for all taxonomic ranks considered. At the same time, a visualization of the projected data permits

102 CHAPTER 8. TAXONOMIC CLASSIFICATION OF DNA FRAGMENTS

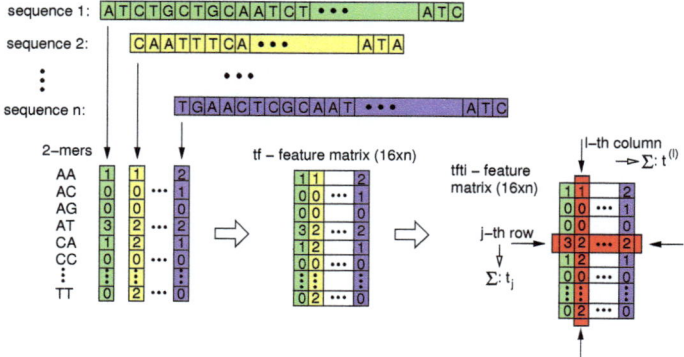

Figure 8.2: In order to find an appropriate representation for the genomic sequences and subsequences, different types of feature vectors are computed: The *term frequency (tf)* feature vector directly consists of the frequencies of oligonucleotide patterns of a specified length (here: $k = 2$) in a sequence. The *term frequency - term importance (tf-ti)* feature vector is based on the *tf* feature vector, but considers the general importance of oligonucleotide patterns – an approach that is similar to the *term frequency - inverse document frequency (tf-idf)* features successfully applied in textmining. Therefore the feature values of those patterns is increased that are rare among all species and that occur more frequently than other patterns in the considered species.

further insights into the data and provides an intuitive browsing through DNA fragment clusters to support the binning process prior to assembly.

8.1 Feature vector computation

In order to allow a comparison between genomic sequences and subsequences (DNA fragments) of different lengths, a representation for each (sub-)sequence has to be found. To this end, feature vectors of a fixed length are computed for each (sub-)sequence that are uniquely based on the nucleotides in the (sub-)sequence. Thus additional information about the (sub-)sequence, which is often difficult or even impossible to obtain for small subsequences, is not required. The entries of the feature vector are computed from the numbers of oligonucleotide patterns of length k in a sliding window of step size one in the forward and reverse DNA strand.

Let Σ be the alphabet of nucleotides $\Sigma = \{A, C, G, T\}$, and let **o** be an oligonucleotide pattern of length $k = |\mathbf{o}|$, with $o_i \in \Sigma$. This results in $|\Sigma|^{|\mathbf{o}|} = 4^k$ possible oligonucleotide patterns of length k, e.g. an oligonu-

8.1. FEATURE VECTOR COMPUTATION

cleotide pattern of length $k = 4$, as used in our experiments, can be one of the following sequences: $\mathbf{o}^{(1)} = AAAA$, $\mathbf{o}^{(2)} = AAAC$, ..., $\mathbf{o}^{(4^k)} = TTTT$. Let $\mathbf{s}^{(l)}$ be the genomic sequence of species l (with $1 \leq l \leq 350$) of length $|s^{(l)}|$ each and $s_i^{(l)} \in \Sigma$.

To find an appropriate representation for the genomic sequences and subsequences, three different types of feature vectors are computed: The *term frequency (tf)* feature vector directly consists of the frequencies of oligonucleotide patterns of a specified length in a sequence. Let $t_j^{(l)}$ be the number of the j-th oligonucleotide (with $j = 1, \ldots, 4^k$) in sequence $\mathbf{s}^{(l)}$. The *tf* feature vector of the genomic sequence of species l is defined as

$$\mathbf{f}_{\text{tf}}^{(l)}(\mathbf{s}^{(l)}) = \left(t_1^{(l)}, t_2^{(l)}, \ldots, t_{4^k}^{(l)}\right)^T \tag{8.1}$$

For illustration see Figure (8.2). The *term frequency - term importance (tf-ti)* feature vector is based on the *tf* feature vector, but considers the general importance of oligonucleotide patterns. This approach is similar to the *term frequency - inverse document frequency (tf-idf)* features successfully applied in the textmining domain (Salton et al., 1975). The traditional *idf* measuring the fraction of documents in which a certain term is contained is not adequate to analyze genomic fragments, because oligonucleotide patterns up to length $k = 6$ are contained in almost every sequence at least once, resulting in an equal importance for each pattern. The importance of an oligonucleotide pattern can be measured by increasing the feature values of those patterns that

1. are rare among all species and that

2. occur more frequently than other patterns in the considered species.

Let $t_j = \sum_{l=1}^{350} t_j^{(l)}$ be the number of the j-th oligonucleotide among all species. Let $t^{(l)} = \sum_{j=1}^{4^k} t_j^{(l)}$ be the number of all oligonucleotides in genomic fragment l (Figure 8.2). The *tf-ti* feature vector of the genomic sequence of species l is defined as

$$\mathbf{f}_{\text{tf-ti}}^{(l)}(\mathbf{s}^{(l)}) = \left(\frac{t_1^{(l)}}{t_1 t^{(l)}}, \frac{t_2^{(l)}}{t_2 t^{(l)}}, \ldots, \frac{t_{4^k}^{(l)}}{t_{4^k} t^{(l)}}\right)^T \tag{8.2}$$

The *oligo* feature vector contains the enhanced contrast between over- and underrepresented oligonucleotide patterns in a sequence. The divergency between expectation and observation of oligonucleotide patterns of length k is given by the ratio of observed vs. expected (Martin et al., 2007). For notation simplicity let us consider only one sequence $\mathbf{s} \equiv \mathbf{s}^{(l)}$ in the following. For a sequence $\mathbf{s}$, the probability to observe a certain nucleotide $\eta \in \Sigma$ can be computed by

$$p(\eta) = \frac{1}{|\mathbf{s}|} \sum_{i=1}^{|\mathbf{s}|} q(s_i, \eta) \qquad (8.3)$$

with the indicator function

$$q(s_i, \eta) = \begin{cases} 1 & \text{if } s_i = \eta \\ 0 & \text{else} \end{cases} \qquad (8.4)$$

The expectation value for a certain oligonucleotide **o** in the sequence **s** can be estimated by

$$E[\mathbf{o}] \approx |\mathbf{s}| \prod_{i=1}^{|\mathbf{o}|} p(o_i) \qquad (8.5)$$

Let $O[\mathbf{o}]$ be the number of observed oligonucleotides **o** in the same sequence **s**. The contrast is performed by computation of the score

$$g(\mathbf{o}) = \begin{cases} 0 & \text{if } O[\mathbf{o}] = 0 \\ \frac{O[\mathbf{o}]}{E[\mathbf{o}]} & \text{if } O[\mathbf{o}] > E[\mathbf{o}] \\ -\frac{E[\mathbf{o}]}{O[\mathbf{o}]} & \text{if } O[\mathbf{o}] \leq E[\mathbf{o}] \end{cases} \qquad (8.6)$$

The *oligo* feature vector of the sequence **s** contains the scores of all possible oligonucleotides:

$$\mathbf{f}_{\text{oligo}}^{(l)}(\mathbf{s}) = \left(g(\mathbf{o}^{(1)}), g(\mathbf{o}^{(2)}), \ldots, g(\mathbf{o}^{(4^k)}) \right)^T \qquad (8.7)$$

8.1.1 Normalization

For further processing in learning algorithms, a normalization of the feature vectors is of decisive importance. The following 12 different normalization strategies have been tested:

Normalization 0: no normalization

Normalization 1: scale all features to unit interval $[0, 1)$

Normalization 2: shift all features to obtain zero mean ($\mu = 0$)

Normalization 3: scale all features to obtain variance ($\sigma^2 = 1$)

Normalization 4: combine normalizations 2 and 3

Normalization 5: scale the data in each feature vector to unit interval

8.1. FEATURE VECTOR COMPUTATION

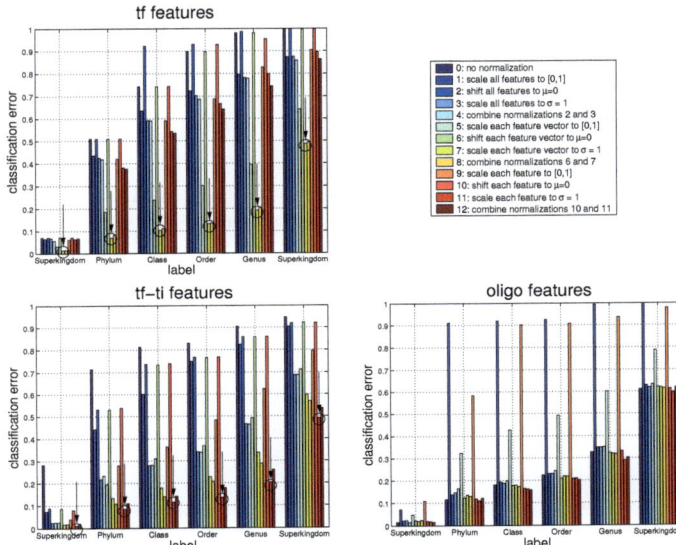

Figure 8.3: A normalization of the feature vectors is of decisive importance for further processing in learning algorithms. 12 different normalization strategies have been tested. The corresponding classification error when classifying DNA fragments of 10 Kb at different ranks is displayed. It can be seen that each type of feature vector works best with its specific normalization strategy. The tf features work best with normalization 7, and the tfti features work best with normalization 11. For the oligo features, no normalization could be found that led to a considerable decrease of the classification error.

Normalization 6: shift the data in each feature vector to obtain zero mean

Normalization 7: scale the data in each feature vector to obtain unit variance

Normalization 8: combine normalizations 6 and 7

Normalization 9: scale each feature among all feature vectors to unit interval

Normalization 10: shift each feature among all feature vectors to zero mean

Normalization 11: scale each feature among all feature vectors to unit variance

Normalization 12: combine normalizations 10 and 11

The classification error obtained when classifying DNA fragments of 10 Kb (Table 8.1, scenario 6) at different ranks is displayed in Figure (8.3). It can be seen that each type of feature vector works best with its specific normalization strategy. The *tf* features work best when the elements of each feature vector are scaled to unit variance (normalization 7), the *tf-ti* features when each component among all vectors is scaled to unit variance (normalization 11). For the *oligo* features, no normalization could be found that led to a considerable decrease of the classification error. The specific best normalization strategies are applied throughout this thesis.

8.2 Results

Hierarchical-growing hyperbolic SOMs (H^{2}SOMs) are trained for classification of normalized feature vectors generated from oligonucleotide patterns of length $k = 4$ of DNA fragments of 350 prokaryotic organisms.[1] The feature vectors, containing either *tf*, *tf-ti*, or *oligo* features, either represent a complete genomic sequence or a genomic subsequence (DNA fragment) of 0.2, 0.5, 1, 3, 5, 10, 15, or 50 Kbp long. In our experimental setting, the genomic subsequences are obtained by cutting them out of the 350 complete sequences (Figure 8.4). A data set primary either consists of 350 feature vectors, each encoding one complete genomic sequence (by adding noise, the data set is enlarged to 2800 feature vectors), or of 2800 feature vectors, computed from eight[2] disjunct genomic subsequences of either 0.2, 0.5, 1, 3, 5, 10, 15 or 50 Kbp of each of the 350 genomic sequences. Even though all 350 genomic sequences are used to generate feature vectors for the training and the testing data set in each scenario, each computed feature vector is either contained in the training or the testing data set, but never in both. A separation of the 350 genomic sequences into training and testing sequences might be an interesting approach at higher ranks, but it is infeasible at rank Species or Genus. A correct classification of a species or genus (which often only consists of one species) becomes impossible if the only existing species has been omitted during training.

The classifier performance is analyzed when training the H^{2}SOM on feature vectors computed from complete genomic sequences and classifying feature

---

[1] no improvement was reported for $k > 4$ - results not shown.
[2] maximal number of disjunct subsequences of 50 Kbp obtainable from any genomic sequence

8.2. RESULTS

scenario	training	→	classification
1.	complete	→	200
2.	complete	→	500
3.	complete	→	1000
4.	complete	→	3000
5.	complete	→	5000
6.	complete	→	10000
7.	complete	→	50000
8.	50000	→	200
9.	50000	→	500
10.	50000	→	1000
11.	50000	→	3000
12.	50000	→	5000
13.	50000	→	10000
14.	10000	→	200
15.	10000	→	500
16.	10000	→	1000
17.	10000	→	3000
18.	10000	→	5000
19.	1000	→	200
20.	1000	→	500

Table 8.1: The H^{2}SOM classifier is trained on feature vectors either representing complete genomic sequences (scenario 1-7) or subsequences of 1-50 Kbp (scenario 8-20) for the classification of shorter genomic subsequences (0.2-50 Kbp).

vectors representing subsequences. (Table 8.1, scenario 1-7). To analyze whether subsequences are also sufficient for training, the H^{2}SOM classifier was also trained on subsequences of 1 to 50 Kbs. (Table 8.1, scenario 8-20). The applied H^{2}SOMs consist of five rings with a branching factor $n_b = 8$, resulting in 2281 nodes. They were trained with 10000 training steps for each ring and a linear decreasing learning rate ($\eta_1 = 0.9$ to $\eta_{10000} = 0.1$) and neighborhood size ($\sigma_1 = 10$ to $\sigma_{10000} = 1$). To address the issue of assigning DNA fragments to their originating species or to bin them for assembly, the DNA fragments are classified at rank superkingdom to species in the tree of life. The classification errors of the H^{2}SOM classifier and the

CHAPTER 8. TAXONOMIC CLASSIFICATION OF DNA FRAGMENTS

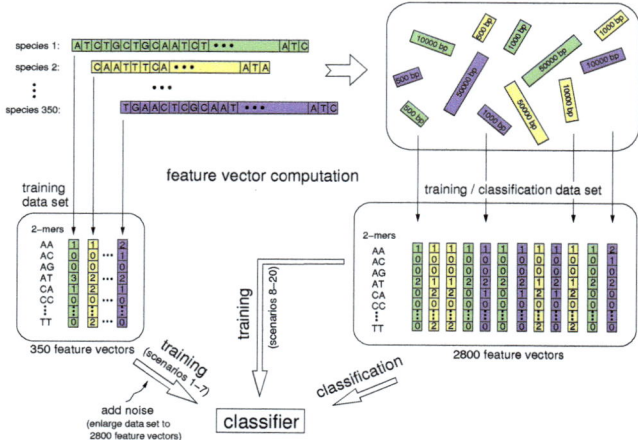

Figure 8.4: Feature vectors, containing either *tf*, *tf-ti*, or *oligo* features, are obtained from either complete genomic sequences or from genomic subsequences of 0.2, 0.5, 1, 3, 5, 10, 15, or 50 Kbp long. In our experimental setting, the genomic subsequences are obtained by cutting them out of the 350 complete sequences. A data set primary either consists of 350 feature vectors, each encoding one complete genomic sequence (by adding noise, the data set is enlarged to 2800 feature vectors), or of 2800 feature vectors, computed from eight disjunct genomic subsequences of either 0.2, 0.5, 1, 3, 5, 10, 15 or 50 Kbp of each of the 350 genomic sequences. Even though all 350 genomic sequences are used to generate feature vectors for the training and the testing data set in each scenario, each computed feature vector is either contained in the training or the testing data set, but never in both.

k-nearest neighbor (knn) classifier[3] (Hastie et al., 2001) at ranks Superkingdom, Phylum, and Class are displayed in Figure (8.5) and those at ranks Order, Genus, and Species are displayed in Figure (8.6) for each training-classification scenario and each type of feature vector. Each scenario was repeated ten times to account for variations in the stochastic learning process.

The figures illustrate that the H^{2}SOM classifies DNA fragments of 0.2-50 kbp with high accuracy to their correct category in the tree of life, but it is still outperformed by the knn classifier. The H^{2}SOM results prove to be relatively stable, only very few outliers were detected. The best results

---

[3] the knn classifier is often used as standard classifier in machine learning

8.2. RESULTS

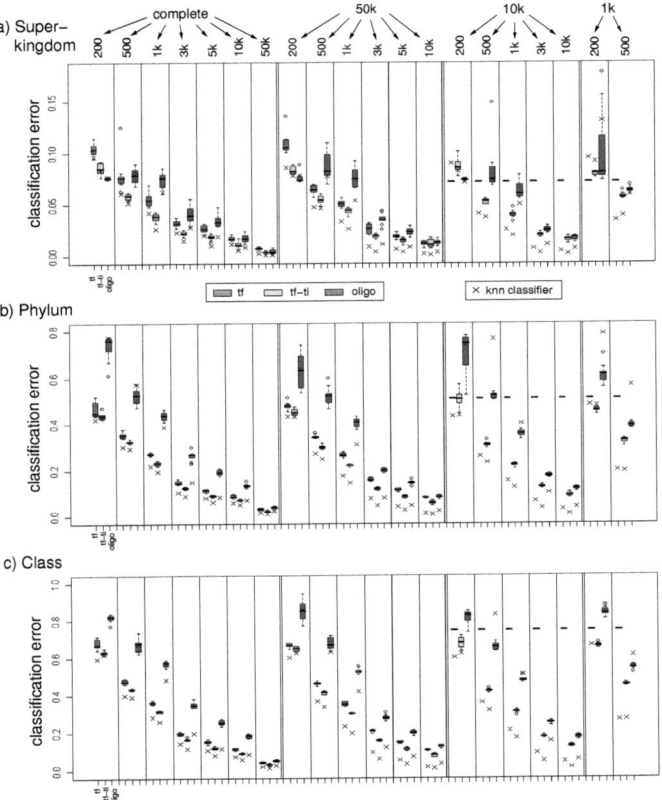

Figure 8.5: Classification errors of the H²SOM and the knn classifier at ranks Superkingdom, Phylum, and Class for each training-classification scenario and each type of feature vector, ten runs each (box-and-whisker plots). It can be seen that the H²SOM classifies small DNA fragments with high accuracy to their correct category in the tree of life, but it is still outperformed by the knn classifier. The H²SOM results prove to be relatively stable, only very few outliers were detected. The best results are obtained for the *complete* → *50 Kb* scenario. Three major observations can be made: First, feature vectors of longer subsequences (50 Kb, 15 Kb, 10 Kb) can be classified more easily than those of shorter subsequences (0.2 Kb, 0.5 Kb, 1 Kb). Second, it seems to be of minor importance whether the H²SOM has been trained on feature vectors from complete sequences, or on subsequences of smaller sizes. Finally, the *tf-ti* feature proves to be the most powerful feature in this context, closely followed by the *tf* feature.

110 CHAPTER 8. TAXONOMIC CLASSIFICATION OF DNA FRAGMENTS

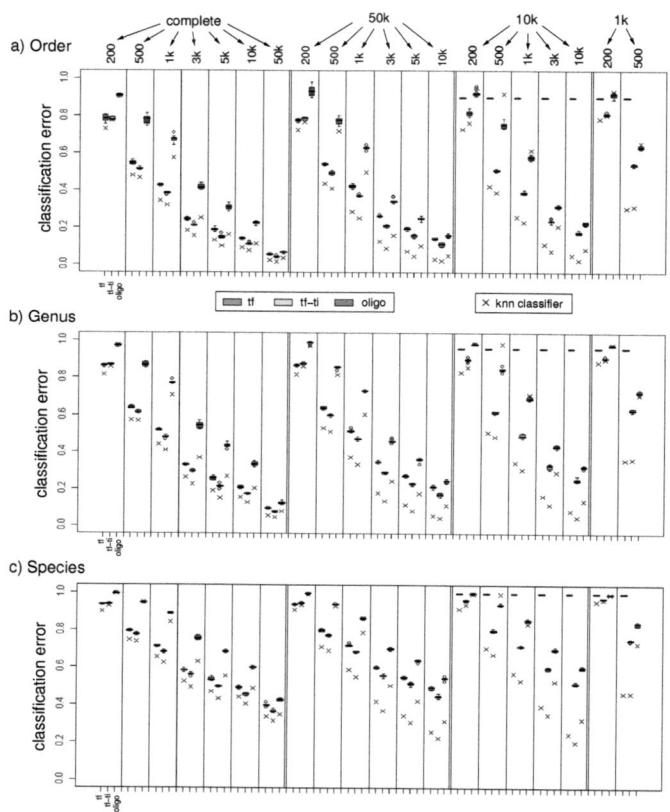

Figure 8.6: Classification errors of the H^2SOM and the knn classifier at ranks Order, Genus, and Species for each training-classification scenario and each type of feature vector, ten runs each (box-and-whisker plots).

8.2. RESULTS

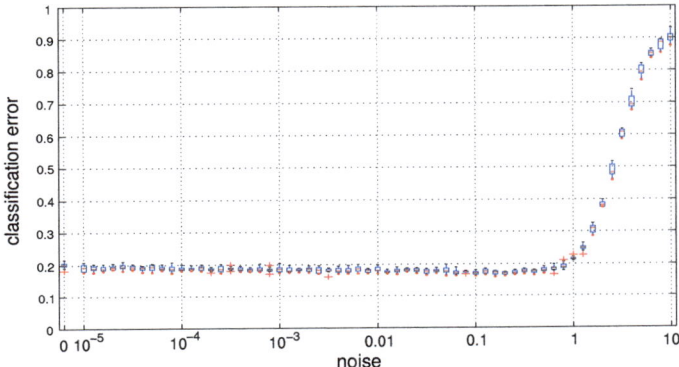

Figure 8.7: Uniformly distributed noise $\eta \in [10^{-5}, 10]$ is added to each component of the 350 feature vectors representing complete sequences and used for training in scenario 1-7. It can be seen that the classification error can be decreased by approximately 10% when noise $\eta \approx 0.2$ is added to each component.

are obtained for the *complete* → *50 Kb* scenario. Three major observations can be made: First, feature vectors of longer subsequences (50 Kb, 15 Kb, 10 Kb) can be easier classified than those of shorter subsequences (0.2 Kb, 0.5 Kb, 1 Kb). Especially for subsequences ≤ 1 Kb the classification error increases considerably. Second, it seems to be of minor importance whether the H²SOM has been trained on feature vectors from complete sequences, or on subsequences of smaller sizes. Finally, the introduced *tf-ti* feature proves to be the most powerful feature in this context, closely followed by the *tf* feature.

In order to enlarge the training data set consisting of 350 feature vectors in scenarios 1 to 7, each feature vector is perturbated with uniformly distributed noise and added to the data set. This scheme is repeated eight times in order to obtain a data set of 2800 items (similar to the data sets of the genomic fragments). Figure (8.7) displays results for scenario 6 at rank genus using *tf-ti* features (ten repetitions). Uniformly distributed noise $\eta \in [10^{-5}, 10]$ is added to each component of the feature vectors. It can be seen that the classification error can be decreased by approximately 10% when noise $\eta \approx 0.2$ is added to each component. Consequently, this amount of noise is subsequently applied throughout the experiments.

Training the H²SOM with feature vectors from 350 species can be performed in less than one minutes on a standard PC with 2 GHz and 256 MB RAM, whereas the classification of the same number of species does not require

112CHAPTER 8. TAXONOMIC CLASSIFICATION OF DNA FRAGMENTS

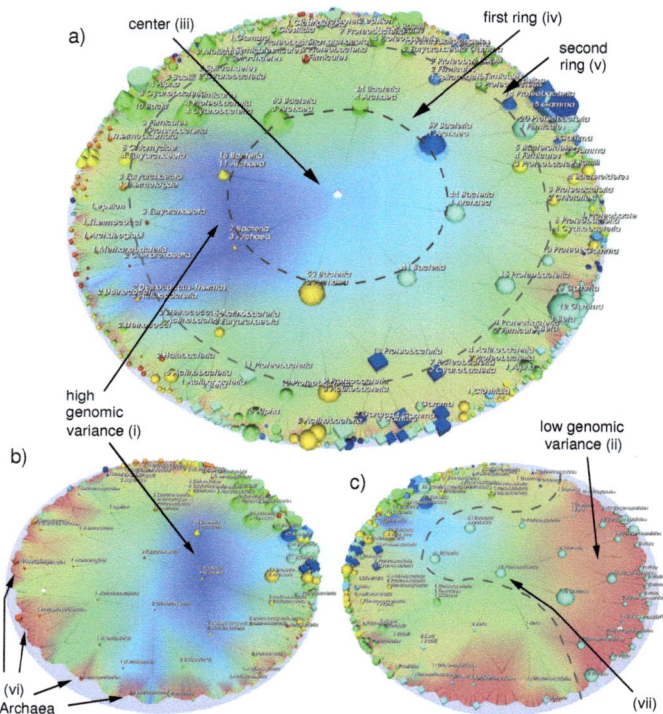

Figure 8.8: The Poincaré projection is used to visualize a trained H²SOM. The background is painted applying to the U-matrix principle: blue areas indicate high node distances in the feature space whereas red ones indicate small node distances. This visualization feature permits to identify regions with high (**i**) and low (**ii**) variation among species. In (**a**) the origin (**iii**) of the HSOM is centered. At each node the most represented taxonomic order is displayed by an order-specific object, colored from red and orange (Archaea) to yellow, green, cyan, and blue (Bacteria), with respect to color code 1 in Figure (3.5). It can be seen, that the species are not randomly mapped to the HSOM nodes, but that taxonomy related species are often mapped close to each other. Additional labels summarize the major content of each node. In the first ring (**iv**), the node content is summarized at rank superkingdom, i.e. it is counted how many Archaea and Bacteria are mapped to each node. In the second ring (**v**), the node content is summarized at rank phylum, i.e. it is counted how many Actinobacteria, Aquificae, and so forth, are mapped to each node. This labeling scheme is continued for the ranks class, order, and genus in the third to fifth ring. The Moebius transformation permits to move any point of the hyperbolic plane to the center in the display while all other points are transformed accordingly (**b** and **c**). Such an interactive browsing and zooming into various regions of the trained HSOM allows to focus on regions of interest. In (**b**) a region containing Archaea (red objects in **vi**) has been dragged towards the center, and in (**c**) a region with Proteobacteria (cyan objects in **vii**) is focused.

more than a few seconds. The knn classifier requires about half a minute for classification.

For visual inspection, a H^{2}SOM trained on the complete genomic data using tf-ti features is displayed using the Poincaré projection (Figure 8.8). The images in Figure (8.8) are generated by the interactive visualization engine as described by Ontrup (2008). The background is painted applying to the U-matrix principle (Ultsch, 1993b): blue areas indicate high node distances in the feature space whereas red ones indicate small node distances. This visualization feature permits to identify regions with high (**i**) and low (**ii**) variation among species. In Figure (8.8a) the origin (**iii**) of the HSOM is centered. At each node the most represented taxonomic order is displayed by an order-specific object, colored from red and orange (Archaea) to yellow, green, cyan, and blue (Bacteria), with respect to color code 1 in Figure (3.5). It can be seen, that the species are not randomly mapped to the HSOM nodes, but that taxonomy related species are often mapped close to each other. Additional labels summarize the major content of each node. In the first ring (**iv**), the node content is summarized at rank superkingdom, i.e. it is counted how many Archaea and Bacteria are mapped to each node. In the second ring (**v**), the node content is summarized at rank phylum, i.e. it is counted how many Actinobacteria, Aquificae, and so forth, are mapped to each node. This labeling scheme is continued for the ranks class, order, and genus in the third to fifth ring. The Moebius transformation permits to move any point of the hyperbolic plane to the center in the display while all other points are transformed accordingly (Figure 8.8b and 8.8c). Such an interactive browsing and zooming into various regions of the trained HSOM allows to focus on regions of interest. In Figure (8.8b) a region containing Archaea (red objects in **vi**) has been dragged towards the center, and in Figure (8.8c) a region with Proteobacteria (cyan objects in **vii**) is focused.

8.3 Feature selection

In order to check if all features (derived from oligonucleotide patterns) in a feature vector are necessary for an accurate classification, a feature selection algorithm is applied to sort the oligonucleotide patterns according to their potential for classification. Experiments for scenario 6 (complete → 10000) and the tf-ti features reveal that 20% of all oligonucleotide patterns are already sufficient to produce similar classification rates at rank genus (Figure 8.9). A slight improvement of the classification rates can even be obtained when half of the oligonucleotide patterns is used. It can also be seen that a classification rate of less than 50% can already be obtained if only patterns up to length 2 are used.

In order to check for stability of the feature selection algorithm, the experiment as shown in Figure (8.9) is repeated ten times for the use of oligonu-

CHAPTER 8. TAXONOMIC CLASSIFICATION OF DNA FRAGMENTS

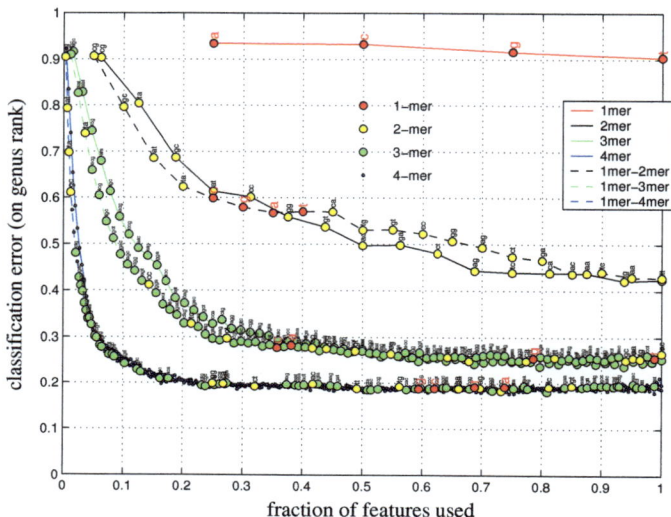

Figure 8.9: A feature selection algorithm is applied for scenario 6 (complete → 10000) and the *tf-ti* features to sort oligonucleotide patterns according to their potential for classification. The solid blue line marks the classification error when features of oligonucleotide patterns of length 4, the dashed blue line when patterns of lengths 1 to 4 are taken into account. Interestingly, the first k-mers selected are cg, at, ta, and gc, indicating their high discriminable power. 20% instead of 100% of all oligonucleotide patterns are already sufficient to produce similar classification rates at rank genus. A slight improvement of the classification rates can even be obtained when half of the oligonucleotide patterns is used. The green, black and red lines mark classification errors for oligonucleotide patterns up to length 3, 2, and 1. It can be seen that a classification rate of less than 50% can already be obtained if only patterns up to length 2 are used.

cleotide patterns up to length 3 (84 features). Figure (8.10) reveals that the classification errors remain relatively stable when running the feature selection algorithm multiple times.

A repetitive run of the feature selection algorithm further allows to rank the oligonucleotide pattern according to their discriminable power for classification. Figure (8.11) shows the results of such an analysis. It can be

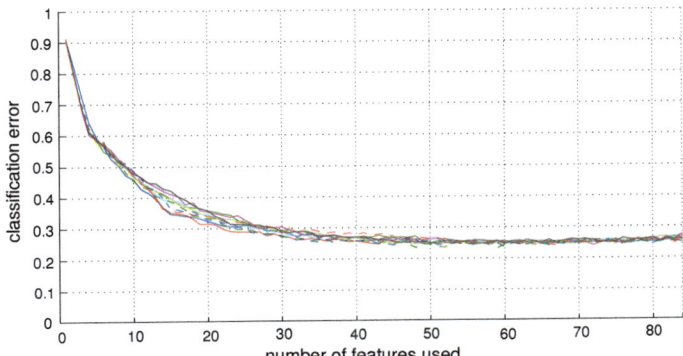

Figure 8.10: A feature selection algorithm is applied ten times for scenario 6 and the *tf-ti* features. Thereby oligonucleotide pattern up to length 3 are used. The classification results at rank genus indicate that the classification errors remain relatively stable when repetitively applying the feature selection algorithm.

seen, that the pattern **cg** has rank 1, which means that it has always been taken as first pattern in each of the ten feature selection experiments. The patterns **at** and **gc** both have rank 3, closely followed by **ta**. The pattern **tct** seems to have least discriminable power for classification. The fact that the oligonucleotide patterns **cg** and **gc** as well as their complementary parts **at** and **ta** are assigned the lowest ranks and thus contain the highes discriminable power for classification confirms the discriminable power of the gc-content in a sequence.

It should be noted that feature selection is computationally expensive. Nevertheless, it offers the opportunity to identify discriminable patterns and therefore helps to improve and to accelerate further classifications when focusing on the identified subset of patterns.

8.4 Discussion

Hierarchical growing hyperbolic SOMs (H^{2}SOMs) were trained for the phylogenetic classification of DNA fragments of 0.2 - 50 Kbp at ranks superkingdom, phylum, class, order, genus, and species. Three different types of feature vectors were applied to represent complete genomic sequences and DNA fragments of 350 prokaryotic organisms. The high classification accuracy at all ranks makes the H^{2}SOM classifier a powerful tool to assign DNA fragments to their originating species or to bin fragments of unknown

CHAPTER 8. TAXONOMIC CLASSIFICATION OF DNA FRAGMENTS

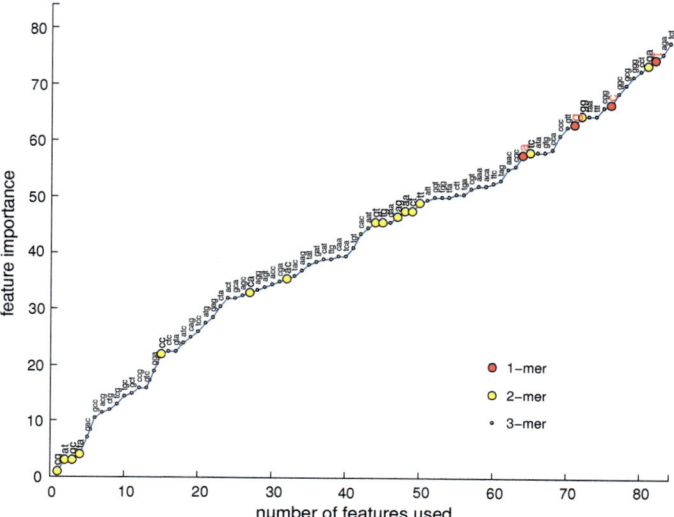

Figure 8.11: A repetitive run of a feature selection algorithm allows to rank the oligonucleotide pattern according to their discriminable power for classification. The pattern cg has rank 1, which means that it has always been taken as first pattern in each of the ten feature selection experiments. The patterns at and gc both have rank 3, closely followed by ta. The pattern tct seems to have least discriminable power for classification. The fact that the oligonucleotide patterns cg and gc as well as their complementary parts at and ta are assigned the lowest ranks and thus contain the highes discriminable power for classification confirms the discriminable power of the gc-content in a sequence.

species for assembly.

Longer DNA fragments are easier to classify, as indicated by their smaller classification errors. The best results are obtained for classification of DNA fragments of 50 Kbp using the *tf-ti* features. Interestingly, the size of the DNA fragments is of minor importance for training, e.g. the classification result for subsequences of 500 bp is almost independent of the (sub-)sequences used for training (complete, 50 Kbp, 10 Kbp, 3 Kbp, or 1 Kbp).

SOMs have the advantage, that they can perform visualization, classification and clustering at the same time. The hierarchical class structure of the considered genomic data motivated the application of a hyperbolic SOM. The

8.4. DISCUSSION

HSOM is organized on a tree grid, but also incorporates links between neighboring branches, which theoretically permit to account for horizontal gene transfer observed in bacteria. For visual inspection, the hyperbolic SOM can be visualized in Euclidean space using the Poincaré projection. Such a visualization allows an easy detection of homogeneous areas and permits to focus on areas of frequent misclassifications for further analysis. A hierarchical training scheme is applied in the hierarchical-growing hyperbolic SOM (H^2SOM) as used throughout our study, allowing considerable speed-ups of several orders of magnitudes compared to the SOM and HSOM. Regarding the classification accuracy, the H^2SOM is still slightly outperformed by the knn classifier. However, the H^2SOM classifier evolves its power with increasing number of sequenced species. The knn classifier requires $O(n)$ time to classify a novel genomic fragment, whereas the H^2SOM classifier needs $O(\log m)$ for the same task when using the ultra-fast tree search, with n being the number of training samples and m being the number of nodes. In addition, the HSOM provides a visualization framework that allows interactive zooming into selected genomic feature space regions on the level of interaction or similar to the hyperbolic tree browser proposed by Lamping et al. (1995). This makes the H^2SOM well suited to deal with the increasing number of sequence reads and sequenced organisms in metagenomic studies and for the testing of different feature spaces or combinations of feature spaces.

To find an appropriate representation of both complete genomes and variable-length DNA fragments, three different feature spaces were analyzed in this study. Even though the tf-ti features produces encouraging results, more sophisticated weighting schemes, combinations of feature spaces, and more complex features based on additional knowledge about oligonucleotide patterns are imaginable. Similar to the research performed in the domain of textmining in the last decade, a new field opens for the development of proper representations of genomic sequences for their automated processing with machine learning applications.

Chapter 9

Reassessing the tree of life using genomic sequences

All existing organisms have evolved from one common ancestor according to the theory of evolution proposed by Darwin (1859). Studying the finches that inhabit the Galapagos archipelago, Darwin envisaged the fact that evolutionary forces can drive the bearing of new species from existing ones. Since then, the ultimate goal of many biologists is to obtain a hierarchical classification or taxonomy able to map the evolutionary relationships between species. Traditionally, evolutionary relationships were established using morphological characteristics (e.g. number of legs), still valid in the analysis of fossil record. However, with the advent of sequencing technologies yielding a vast amount of molecular data, it has become possible to reassess the relationship between species (Zuckerkandl and Pauling, 1965). The evolutionary relationship between all existing species can be modeled and visualized by the "tree like structure" which is known as the *tree of life* (Figure 3.4).

Using sequence alignment molecular biologists can estimate the differences between DNA sequences of certain species of interest, in order to estimate the degree of their relationship, namely sequence similarity (the closer their relationship the more similar they should be). Conventionally, only part of the genome (often a single gene) is used for this purpose such as ribosomal RNA molecules, gene content, gene order, protein domain content, etc. However, many pitfalls in sequence alignment can be encountered such as saturation of the underlying model of evolution (when far related species are compared), sampling of representative sequences, lateral gene transfer, or recombination. All these lead to very disparate results (Brocchieri, 2001). Moreover, multiple sequence alignments are computationally very expensive.

Nowadays, with the gargantuan amount of molecular information it is very valuable to count on methods that can make use of the information contained in the whole genome and do not depend on sequence alignment, but nevertheless can readily reconstruct the relationship between species and help in the evaluation of trends in genome evolution. New alignment-free approaches that take into account general characteristics of the genomes disregarding prior identification of functional regions have been developed (Gupta, 1998; Stuart et al., 2002; Qi et al., 2004; Chapus et al., 2005). But this is still a challenge in computational biology. An intriguing characteristic that enables to capture evolutionary relationships between species is the genomic signature which is defined as the whole set of short sequences of oligonucleotide of certain length (Karlin and Burge, 1995). Genomic signatures are species-specific and can be measured in any part of the genome (Deschavanne et al., 1999; Abe et al., 2002, 2005) allowing direct comparisons along the entire genome.

In this chapter, the suitability of several SOMs for reconstructing the hierarchical relation of whole genomic sequences is explored. Hereby, compositional sequence properties (genomic signature) are exploited. One way to find an answer is to apply dimension reduction techniques based on unsupervised learning like the SOM, to learn and project the structure of a large set of genomic signatures. Our data set of 350 organisms represents a vast majority of organisms sequenced up-to-date from the two domains of life. Genomic signatures are uniquely obtained from each complete sequenced genome without using any additional knowledge about the organisms. For each organism, the features are combined in a vector that is used to train a SOM in Euclidean and hyperbolic space. It is evaluated if the structure recovered from the different SOMs reflects the gold standard of current taxonomy. Results are presented for the SOM, HSOM and H^{2}SOM. By comparing ranks of distances in the feature space, on the grid and in the tree of life, it is shown that the structure of the trained SOMs using only whole genome sequence data is biologically sound to the widely accepted *tree of life* based on RNA molecules. When the distances are directly compared, both the HSOM and H^{2}SOM perform better than the standard SOM, which makes them better suited for embedding of the high dimensional genomic signatures. Additionally, the H^{2}SOM allows considerable speed-ups of several orders of magnitudes which makes it well suited to deal with the increasing number of sequenced organisms and for the testing of different feature spaces.

9.1 Material and methods

In this chapter, the 350 prokaryotic organisms as described in section 3.2.5 are considered. This represents a vast majority of sequenced organisms from the two domains archaea and bacteria. For each complete genomic sequence representing a genome, the oligo features (section 8.1) are computed for oligonucleotide lengths 2 to 6.

In order to evaluate if the structure recovered from different SOMs reflect the gold standard of current taxonomy, point-to-point distances in the feature space, on the SOM grid and in the tree of life are analyzed. The correlation between distances, or Spearman's ρ when applied to distances can measure to which extent the distances of point pairs in two different spaces $\mathcal{S}^1$ and $\mathcal{S}^2$ are correlated (section 2.4.4). In this work, distances between organisms are computed in three different ways. First, the *feature space distance* $d_{ij}^f \in [0,1]$ can be obtained by computing the Euclidean distance $d\left(f\left(\mathbf{s}^{(i)}\right), f\left(\mathbf{s}^{(j)}\right)\right)$ between two organisms i and j in the feature space and normalizing it to [0,1]. Second, a *grid distance* $d_{ij}^g \in [0,1]$ can be obtained by computing the minimal distance on the SOM grid between the two nodes to which the organisms i and j have been mapped. The grid distances are normalized such that the maximal possible distance on the grid is one. Third, the *taxonomy distance* $d_{ij}^t \in [0,1]$ of two organisms i and j is defined as follows:

$$d_{ij}^t = \begin{cases} 0 & \text{if they have the genus in common} \\ 0.2 & \text{if they have the class in common} \\ 0.4 & \text{if they have the order in common} \\ 0.6 & \text{if they have the phylum in common} \\ 0.8 & \text{if they have the superkingdom in common} \\ 1 & \text{if they have nothing in common} \end{cases}$$

9.2 Results

A standard SOM, a HSOM, and a H²SOM are trained on the data described in section 3.2.5. The features are defined by oligonucleotides of length k ranging between 2 and 6 in five different data sets. All SOMs are trained with 10000 training steps and a linear decreasing learning rate ($\eta_1 = 0.9$ to $\eta_{10000} = 0.1$) and neighborhood size ($\sigma_1 = 10$ to $\sigma_{10000} = 1$). All hyperbolic SOMs consist of five rings with a branching factor $n_b = 8$, resulting in 2281 nodes. The standard SOM is initialized using the eigenvectors of the first and second largest eigenvalue. Its dimension is determined by the relation between the first and second largest eigenvalue such that the number of nodes is approximately the same as in the hyperbolic SOMs. For each data set and for each training algorithm, the SOMs are trained 10 times.

The following two issues are analyzed: To which extent does the structure of the grid correspond to *i)* the structure in the feature space, and *ii)* the taxonomy? To this end, the correlations between distances (section 2.4.4) and correlations between ranks of distances using Spearman's ρ (section 2.4.4) are analyzed.

In Figure (9.1) Spearman's ρ between feature space distances and grid distances is displayed. A $\rho \approx 0.6$ indicates that the ranks of distances are very

9.2. RESULTS

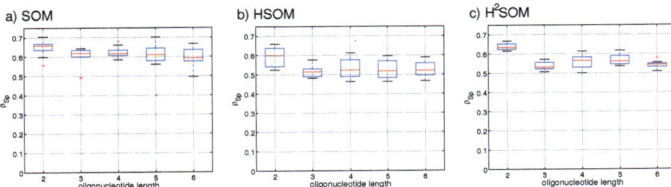

Figure 9.1: Spearman's ρ between feature space distances and grid distances is displayed. A $\rho \approx 0.6$ indicates that the ranks of distances are very well preserved. This observation is rather independent of the oligonucleotide length and the SOM used.

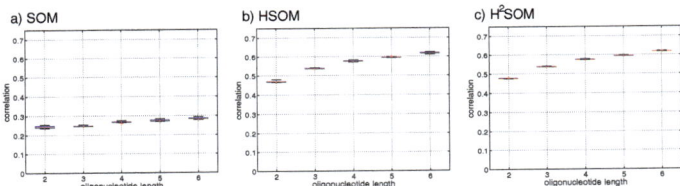

Figure 9.2: The correlation between feature space distances and grid distances is shown. It can be seen that SOMs in hyperbolic space better preserve the distances than the SOM in Euclidean space. The performance of the SOMs increases with the oligonucleotide length.

well preserved. This observation is rather independent of the oligonucleotide length and the SOM used. When considering the direct correlation of feature space distances and grid distances Figure (9.2), the SOMs in hyperbolic space better preserve the distances than the SOM in Euclidean space. The performance of the SOMs increases with the oligonucleotide length.

The difference between Spearman's ρ and the direct correlation can be explained by the different distributions of distances on the SOM grid. In Euclidean space the distribution of node distances favors smaller distances whereas in the hyperbolic case the exponential scaling behavior of $I\!H^2$ allows a larger proportion of the nodes to have a rather large distance to each other. This feature allows the hyperbolic SOM to better reflect the true distribution of distances in the original high dimensional oligonucleotide space.

In Figure (9.3) Spearman's ρ between grid distances and taxonomy distances is shown. The slight positive ρ_{Sp} indicates that there is a link between the structure found by the SOMs and the taxonomy.

When considering the direct correlation between grid distances and tax-

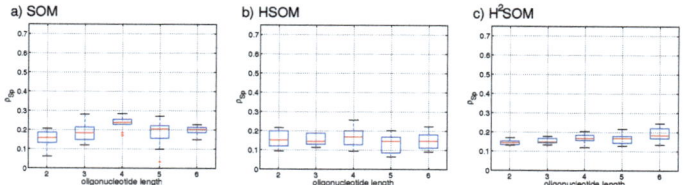

Figure 9.3: Spearman's ρ between grid distances and taxonomy distances is shown. The slight positive ρ_{Sp} indicates that there is a link between the structure found by the SOMs and the taxonomy.

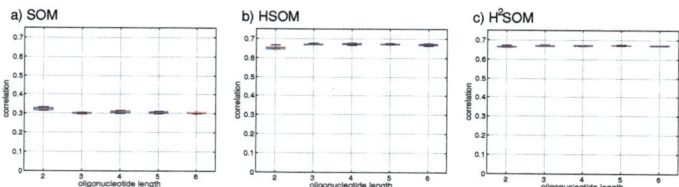

Figure 9.4: The correlation between grid distances and taxonomy distances is displayed. The SOMs in hyperbolic space preserve the distances better than the SOM in Euclidean space. This observation is independent of the oligonucleotide length.

onomy distances (Figure 9.4), the SOMs in hyperbolic space preserve the distances better than the SOM in Euclidean space. This observation is independent of the oligonucleotide length. For visual inspection, a randomly chosen HSOM trained with oligonucleotides of length 4 and organisms colored according to their position in the taxonomy tree is displayed using the Poincaré projection (Figure 9.5). In Figure (9.5a) the origin of the $I\!H^2$ is centered. In Figures (9.5b) to (9.5e) different nodes of the HSOM (21, 39, 19, 1) are moved to the center of the display. All other points of the $I\!H^2$ are moved accordingly allowing us to inspect various regions in the hyperbolic space. The organisms are visualized as colored circles at the node to which they are mapped. Each color represents a genus given by color code 2 in Figure (3.5). The circle area is proportional to the number of species that are mapped to the node, but also decreases with the distance to the center node. It can be seen that organisms are not randomly mapped to the HSOM nodes, but that taxonomy related organisms are often mapped close to each other.

9.2. RESULTS

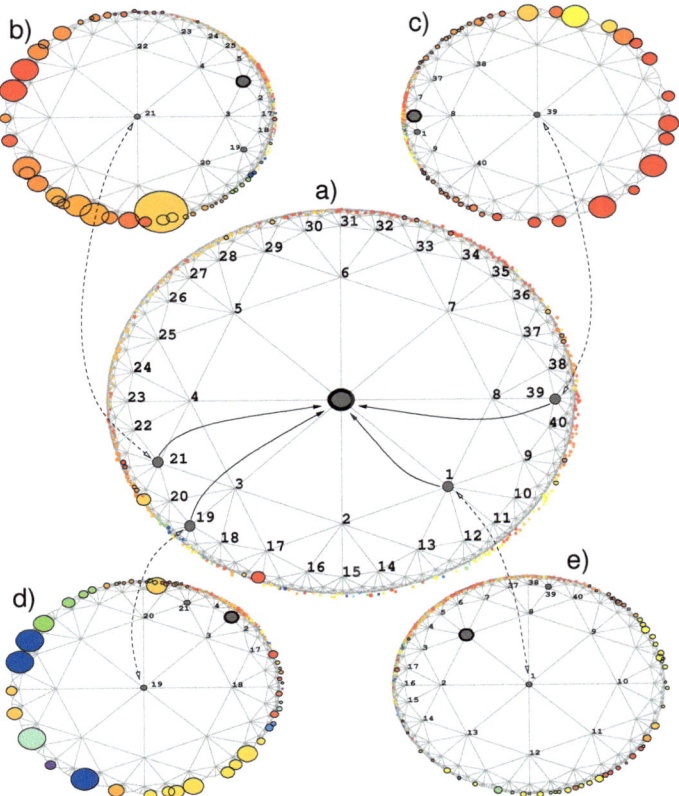

Figure 9.5: For visual inspection, a randomly chosen HSOM trained with oligonucleotides of length 4 and organisms colored according to their position in the taxonomy tree is displayed using the Poincaré projection. In (a) the origin of the $I\!H^2$ is centered. In (b) to (e) different nodes of the HSOM (21, 39, 19, 1) are moved to the center of the display. All other points of the $I\!H^2$ are moved accordingly allowing us to inspect various regions in the hyperbolic space. The organisms are visualized as colored circles at the node to which they are mapped. Each color represents a genus given by color code 2 in Figure (3.5). The circle area is proportional to the number of species that are mapped to the node, but also decreases with the distance to the center node. It can be seen that organisms are not randomly mapped to the HSOM nodes, but taxonomy related organisms are often mapped close to each other.

9.3 Summary and discussion

A standard SOM in Euclidean space, a hyperbolic SOM (HSOM) and a hierarchical hyperbolic SOM (H^2SOM) is applied on genomic signatures of 350 different organisms of the two superkingdoms Bacteria and Archaea. The three different types of SOMs are evaluated by comparing Spearman's ρ and correlations of feature space distances, grid distances and taxonomy distances. The oligo features, which are relatively simple simple features obtained from genomic signatures, are sufficient to allow a reasonable SOM projection. By comparing Spearman's ρ and correlations of distances in the feature space, on the grid and in the tree of life, if is shown that the structure of the trained SOMs using complete genome sequence data is biologically sound to the widely accepted tree of life based on RNA molecules. When the distances are directly compared, both the HSOM and H^2SOM perform better than the standard SOM, which makes the hyperbolic SOMs better suited for visualization issues. Additionally, the H^2SOM allows considerable speed-ups of several orders of magnitudes. This makes it well suited to deal with the increasing number of sequenced organisms and for the testing of different feature spaces or combinations of feature spaces.

Chapter 10
Conclusion

In this thesis, visual data mining techniques for the analysis of intrinsic hierarchical complex biodata are developed. Application of these methods is presented for gene expression data in biomedicine as well as for sequence data in metagenomics. Complex biological data is characterized by a high dimensionality, multi-modality, missing values and noisiness. This confronts the researcher with the difficult question of how to analyze the data in an integrative manner to extract a maximal amount of useful information. A manual evaluation of the complete data is usually infeasible, and an automated analysis is only applicable to a limited extend. In this thesis, tools for an interactive data analysis are developed that permit an integration of the researcher's intuition and background knowledge. Biological data often has an intrinsic hierarchical structure (e.g. tumor types, or species in the Tree of Life), a feature that should be considered when developing novel approaches for complex data analysis. Methods for both cluster validation and the enhancement of visualized clustering results have been developed which led to several advances in the fields of gene expression analysis, sequence analysis and metagenomics.

A *Tree Index* has been developed that externally validates hierarchical clustering results obtained by hierarchical agglomerate clustering (chapter 5). The Tree Index is the first cluster index for hierarchical clustering results. Its high performance has been demonstrated on artificial and real-world microarray data. An extension to the Tree Index, the *Normalized Tree Index* has been developed to identify correlations between clustered data and external labels (chapter 6). In contrast to traditional correlation coefficients, it allows to quantify the correlations between nominal clinical parameters and the *complete* microarray data. A visual display, the *REEFSOM*, has been adapted to integrate clustered gene expression data with clinical and categorical data (chapter 7). The resulting images are both informative and entertaining and can be interpreted easily. Their visual inspection enables to uncover interesting structural patterns in microarray, clinical and categorical data.

In the field of sequence analysis and metagenomics, the following advances have been made: A SOM classifier in hyperbolic space has been developed to classify small variable-length DNA fragments of 350 prokaryotic organisms at six taxonomic levels in the Tree of Life (chapter 8). Thereby, highly discriminable features for genomic sequences have been developed. Finally, studies about the capacities of SOMs to reassess the structural organization of the prokaryotic organisms in the Tree of Life were performed in both Euclidean and hyperbolic space (chapter 9).

10.1 Future prospects

Novel technologies, low-priced storage capacities and computer networking lead to complex data in various domains. The amount of data that is available for one subject of interest will probably continuously increase as time and research progress. The potential to obtain fundamental insights into different aspects of life will increase with the amount and diversity of available data. A central question is and will be to analyze the multi-modal high-dimensional data in an integrative manner to extract a maximal amount of information from it. To achieve such an integrative analysis, novel data-driven approaches for understanding complex data have been developed in this thesis. Even though tested in the context of human gene expression data analysis and sequence analysis, the novel approaches are not limited to these fields of research. They can be extended to address further challenges in biomedicine as well as in other fields of research. The (Normalized) Tree Index is a help tool for the validation of clustering results when dealing with microarray data from any human tissue, other eukaryotes or prokaryotes. Also, with the expansion of databases for gene annotation and gene ontology (Mewes et al., 2002; GO-Consortium, 2000), a validation of clustered genes according to their functions in various pathways will become possible. To this end, the (Normalized) Tree Index has to be extended for a validation of multi-variate external labels as they arise when genes are considered to be involved in more than one function of a pathway. The application of hierarchical cluster algorithms is not limited to the analysis of gene expression data. In proteomics, metabolomics and other *omics*-domains the validation of clustered data is just as important.

In this thesis, metagenomic studies have only been performed on prokaryotic sequences. An application on human or other eukaryotic sequence data has the potential to obtain revolutionary insights into life, categorizations of species and variations between them. The number of sequenced eukaryotic organisms is still limited, but it will increase considerably within the next decade.

Further investigations on horizontal gene transfer should by performed by

10.1. FUTURE PROSPECTS

the H^{2}SOM. Its structure and its training algorithm allows us to group species on different level in a hierarchy while - at the same time - relations between species on equal levels but of different branches can be represented.
Some basic features have been developed for a proper representation of genomic sequences (chapter 8). The development of novel sophisticated features that take background knowledge of researchers into account is a fundamental step to further improve the results of machine learning algorithms in biomedicine.

List of Figures

1.1	Complex data	2
2.1	Spectral clustering	11
2.2	The Self-Organizing Map (SOM)	14
2.3	SOM learning	15
2.4	The Torus SOM	17
2.5	The hierarchically growing hyperbolic SOM (H^2SOM)	18
2.6	Topographic error	20
2.7	Trustworthiness	22
3.1	DNA Microarray technology	33
3.2	Normalizing intensities using lowess function	34
3.3	Visualization of clustered microarray data and clinical data	35
3.4	Phylogenetic tree	36
3.5	The Tree of Life	37
4.1	Intra- and inter-cluster variance	40
4.2	Sharp and blurred clusters	41
4.3	Index I and Separation	42
4.4	Silhouette Width	43
4.5	Dunn's Index	44
4.6	Sensitivity, Specificity, Neg./Pos. predictive value, False Pos./Neg. Rate	46
5.1	Characteristics of appealing and non-appealing cluster trees	53
5.2	Inspection of one single split in a cluster tree	54
5.3	Cluster trees and histograms with a high, mediocre, and low Tree Index	55
5.4	The hypergeometric distribution	56
5.5	The TI applied on four perturbated artificial data sets	59
5.6	The cluster tree with highest TI of the van de Vijver breast cancer data set	61
5.7	The cluster tree with a mediocre TI of the van de Vijver breast cancer data set	62

LIST OF FIGURES

5.8	The cluster tree with highest TI of the multi-class Ramaswamy data set	64
5.9	The cluster tree with a mediocre TI of the multi-class Ramaswamy data set	65
5.10	Tree structures and leaf orderings	70
5.11	The cumulative hypergeometric distribution	71
6.1	Computing the correlation between clinical parameters and microarray data	74
6.2	Lower and upper bound for the TI	76
6.3	Computation of an empirical p-value for the NTI	77
6.4	Summary of NTIs for van de Vijver and Bielefeld data set	83
6.5	Evaluation of the van de Vijver data set (1)	84
6.6	Evaluation of the van de Vijver data set (2)	85
6.7	Evaluation of the Bielefeld data set (1)	86
6.8	Evaluation of the Bielefeld data set (2)	87
6.9	Evaluation of the Bielefeld data set (3)	88
7.1	The fish glyph GUI	92
7.2	A flight into the REEFSOM	93
7.3	Single Fish	96
7.4	Visualization of a complete REEFSOM	98
8.1	Classifying DNA fragments at different phylogenetic ranks	100
8.2	Feature vector computation	102
8.3	Feature vector normalizations	105
8.4	Data set generation and classification scheme	108
8.5	Classification errors at ranks Superkingdom, Phylum, and Class	109
8.6	Classification errors at ranks Order, Genus, and Species	110
8.7	Increasing the classification performance by noise adding	111
8.8	Visualizing a trained H^2SOM using the Poincaré projection (1)	112
8.9	Feature selection	114
8.10	Stability of feature selection results	115
8.11	Revealing the discriminable power of oligonucleotide patterns using feature selection	116
9.1	Spearman's ρ between feature space distances and grid distances	121
9.2	Correlation between feature space distances and grid distances	121
9.3	Spearman's ρ between grid distances and taxonomy distances	122
9.4	Correlation between grid distances and taxonomy distances	122
9.5	Visualizing a trained H^2SOM using the Poincaré projection (2)	123

List of Tables

3.1 (Dis-)advantages of Sanger technique and 454 pyrosequencing   28

5.1 Number of tree structures and leaf orderings   63

6.1 Clinical parameters of the van de Vijver data set   78
6.2 Clinical parameters of the Bielefeld data set (1)   79
6.3 Clinical parameters of the Bielefeld data set (2)   80

7.1 Mapping clinical and categorical features to the parameters of the fish glyph   95

8.1 Training-classification scenarios for H^2SOM classifier   107

Bibliography

Abe, T., Kanaya, S., Kinouchi, M., Ichiba, Y., Kozuki, T., and Ikemura, T. (2002). A novel bioinformatic strategy for unveiling hidden genome signatures of eukaryotes: self-organizing map of oligonucleotide frequency. *Genome Inform*, 13:12–20.

Abe, T., Shigehiko, K., Kennosuke, W., and Ikemuraa, T. (2007). Characterization of Genetic Signal Sequences with Batch-Learning SOM. *Proceedings of the 6th International Workshop on Self-Organizing Maps (WSOM 2007)*.

Abe, T., Sugawara, H., Kanaya, S., and Ikemura, T. (2006). A novel bioinformatics tool for phylogenetic classification of genomic sequence fragments derived from mixed genomes of uncultured environmental microbes. *Polar Biosci*, 20:103–122.

Abe, T., Sugawara, H., Kinouchi, M., Kanaya, S., and Ikemura, T. (2005). Novel phylogenetic studies of genomic sequence fragments derived from uncultured microbe mixtures in environmental and clinical samples. *DNA Res*, 12(5):281–290.

Alexa, M. and Müller, W. (1998). Visualization by metamorphosis. In Wittenbrink, C. M. and Varshney, A., editors, *IEEE Visualization 1998 Late Breaking Hot Topics Proceedings*, pages 33–36.

Allison, D., Cui, X., Page, G., and Sabripour, M. (2006). Microarray data analysis: from disarray to consolidation and consensus. *Nat Rev Genet.*, 7:55–65.

Azuaje (2005). *Data analysis and visualization in genomics and proteomics*. Wiley.

Bach, F. R. and Jordan, M. I. (2004). Learning spectral clustering. In Thrun, S., Saul, L., and Schölkopf, B., editors, *Advances in Neural Information Processing Systems 16*. MIT Press, Cambridge, MA.

Bar-Joseph, Z., Gifford, D. K., and Jaakkola, T. S. (2001). Fast optimal leaf ordering for hierarchical clustering. *Bioinformatics*, 17, Suppl 1:S22–9.

Bengio, Y., Vincent, P., Paiement, J.-F., Delalleau, O., Ouimet, M., and Roux, N. L. (2003). Spectral clustering and kernel pca are learning eigenfunctions. Technical Report 1239, Département d'informatique et recherche opérationnelle, Université de Montréal.

Bezdek, J. and Pal, N. (1995). An index of topological preservation for feature extraction. *Pattern Recognition*, 28(3):381–391.

Bishop, C. (2007). *Pattern Recognition and Machine Learning*. Springer.

Bittner, M., Meltzer, P., and et al. (2000). Molecular classification of cutaneous malignant melanoma by gene expression profiling. *Nature*, 406:536–540.

Bolshakova, N. and Azuaje, F. (2005). Estimating the number of clusters in DNA microarray data. *Methods of Information in Medicine*.

Bolshakova, N. and Azuaje, F. (2006). Estimating the number of clusters in DNA microarray data. *Methods Inf Med.*, 45(2):153–157.

Bolshakova, N., Azuaje, F., and Cunningham, P. (2005). An integrated tool for microarray data clustering and cluster validity assessment. *Bioinformatics*, 21(4):451–455.

Brennan, D. J. (2005). Application of DNA microarray technology in determining breast cancer prognosis and therapeutic response. *Expert opinion on biological therapy*, 5(8):1069–83.

Brocchieri, L. (2001). Phylogenetic inferences from molecular sequences: review and critique. *Theor Popul Biol*, 59(1):27–40.

Calinski, R. and Harabasz, J. (1974). A dendrite method for cluster analysis. *Comm. in Statistics*, 3:1–27.

Chapus, C., Dufraigne, C., Edwards, S., Giron, A., and Fertil, B Deschavanne, P. (2005). Exploration of phylogenetic data using a global sequence analysis method. *BMC Evol Biol*, 5:63.

Charless Fowlkes, Serge Belongie, Fan Chung, and Jitendra Malik (2004). Spectral Grouping Using the Nyström Method. *IEEE PAMI*, 26(2):214–25.

Chen, G., Jaradat, S. A., et al. (2002). Evaluation and comparison of clustering algorithms in analyzing ES cell gene expression data. *Statistica Sinica*, 12:241–62.

Cheng, Y. and Church, G. (2000). Biclustering of expresssion data. *Proceedings ISMB*, pages 93–103.

Chernoff, H. (1971). The use of faces to represent points in n-dimensional pace graphically. Technical Report RN NR-042-993, Dept. of Stat., Stanford Univ.

Cho, H., Dhillon, I., Guan, Y., and Sra, S. (2004). Minimum sum squared residue co-clustering of gene expression data.

Chua, M. and Eick, S. (1998). Information rich glyphs for software management. *IEEE Computer Graphics and Applications*, 18:24–9.

Cleveland, W. S. (1979). Robust locally weighted regression and smoothing scatterplots. *Journal of the American Statistical Association*, 74:829–836.

Cleveland, W. S. and Devlin, S. J. (1988). Locally weighted regression: An approach to regression analysis by local fitting. *Journal of the American Statistical Association*, 83:596–610.

Darwin, C. (1859). *On the Origin of Species by Means of Natural Selection, or the Preservation of Favoured Races in the Struggle for Life*. John Murray.

Datta, S. and Datta, S. (2006). Methods for evaluating clustering algorithms for gene expression data using a reference set of functional classes. *BMC Bioinf.*, 7(397).

Davies, D. and Bouldin, D. (1979). A cluster separation measure. *IEEE Trans. Pattern Recogn. Machine Intell.*, 1:224–7.

de Bodt, E., Cottrell, M., and Verleysen, M. (2002). Statistical tools to assess the reliability of self-organizing maps. *Neural Networks, Special Issue*, 15:967–978.

Deschavanne, P. J., Giron, A., Vilain, J., Fagot, G., and Fertil, B. (1999). Genomic signature: characterization and classification of species assessed by chaos game representation of sequences. *Mol Biol Evol*, 16(10):1391–1399.

Dettling, M. and Buehlmann, P. (2004). Finding predictive gene groups from microarray data. *Journal of Multivariate Analysis*, 90(1):106–31.

Dhillon, I., Fan, J., and Guan, Y. (2001). Efficient clustering of very large document collections. In Grossman, R., Kamath, G., , and Naburu, R., editors, *Data Mining for Scientific and Engineering Applications*. Kluwer Academic Publishers.

Ding, C. (2002). Analysis of gene expression profiles: class discovery and leaf ordering. In *Proc. RECOMB 2002*.

Dorling, D. (1994). Cartograms for visualizing human geography. In Hearnshaw, H. M. and Unwin, D. J., editors, *Visualization in geographical Information Systems*, pages 85–102, Chichester. John Wiley & Sons.

du Toit, S., Steyn, A., and et al. (1986). *Graphical exploratory data analysis*. Springer.

BIBLIOGRAPHY

Duda, R. O., Hart, P. E., and Stork, D. G. (2001). *Pattern Classification*. John Wiley and Sons, Inc., New York.

Dudoit, S. and Fridlyand, J. (2002). A prediction-based resampling method for estimating the number of clusters in a dataset. *Genome Biol.*, 3:research0036.1–0036.21.

Dunn, J. (1974). Well separated clusters and optimal fuzzy partitions. *J. Cybernetics*, 4:95–104.

Eisen, M. B., Spellman, P. T., Brown, P. O., and Botstein, D. (1998). Cluster analysis and display of genome-wide expression patterns. *PNAS*, 95:14863–8.

Famili, A. F., Liu, G., and Liu, Z. (2004). Evaluation and optimization of clustering in gene expression data analysis. *Bioinformatics*, 20(10):1535–1545.

Fischer, I. (2005). Amplifying the block matrix structure for spectral clustering. In van Otterlo, M., Poel, M., and Nijholt, A., editors, *Proceedings of the 14th Annual Machine Conference of Belgium and the Netherlands : BENELEARN Jan. 2005; Poland*, pages 21–8.

Fischer, I. and Poland, J. (2004). New methods for spectral clustering. Technical Report No. IDSIA-12-04; Dalle Molle Institute for Artificial Intelligence; Galleria 2, 6928 Manno, Switzerland.

Fisher, R. A. (1915). Frequency distribution of the values of the correlation coefficient in samples from an indefinitely large population. *Biometrika*, 10(4):507–521.

Fologea, D. and et al. (2005). Detecting single stranded dna with a solid state nanopore. *Nano Lett.*, 5(10):1905–9.

Fraser, C. M. and Fleischmann, R. D. (1997). Strategies for whole microbial genome sequencing and analysis. *Electrophoresis*, 18:1207Ü1216.

Gasch, A. P. and Eisen, M. B. (2002). Exploring the conditional coregulation of yeast gebe expression though fuzzy k-means clustering. *Genome Biol.*, 3:1–22.

Gat-Viks, I., Sharan, R., and Shamir, R. (2003). Scoring clustering solutions by their biological relevance. *Bioinformatics*, 19(18):2381–2389.

Getz, G. and et al. (2000). Coupled two-way clustering analysis of gene microarray data. *PNAS*, 97(22):12079–84.

GO-Consortium (2000). The Gene Ontology Consortium; Gene Ontology: tool for the unification of biology. *Nat. Gene.*, 25:25–29.

Golub, A. D. and et al. (1999). Molecular classification of cancer, class discovery and class prediction by gene expression. *Science*, 286:531–537.

Goodman, L. and Kruskal, W. (1954). Measures of associations for cross-validations. *J. Am. Stat. Assoc.*, 49:732–764.

Gordon, A. (1980). *Classification*. Chapman & Hall, London.

Gu, M., Zha, H., Ding, C., He, X., and Simon, H. (2001). Spectral relaxation models and structure analysis for k-way graph clustering and bi-clustering. *Technical report, Penn. State Univ, Computer Science and Engineering*.

Gupta, R. S. (1998). Protein phylogenies and signature sequences: A reappraisal of evolutionary relationships among archaebacteria, eubacteria, and eukaryotes. *Microbiol Mol Biol Rev*, 62(4):1435–1491.

Halkidi, M., Batistakis, Y., and Vazirgiannis, M. (2001). On clustering validation techniques. *Journal of Intelligent Information Systems*, 17(2-3):107–145.

Handelsmann, J., Tiedje, J. M., and et al. (2007). *The New Science of Metagenomics: Revealing the Secrets of Our Microbial Planet*. The National Academies Press, Washington, DC.

Handl, J., Knowles, J., and Kell, D. B. (2005). Computational cluster validation in post-genomic data analysis. *Bioinformatics*, 21(15):3201–3212.

Hartigan, J. (1975a). Printergraphics for clustering. *ournal. of Statistical Computing and Simulation*, 4:187–213.

Hartigan, J. A. (1975b). *Clustering Algorithms*. Wiley.

Hastie, T., Tibshirani, R., and Friedman, J. (2001). *The Elements of Statistical Learning Data Mining, Inference, and Prediction*. Springer Series in Statistics. Springer. Fondi di Ricerca Salvatore Ruggieri - Numero 555 d'inventario.

Honkela, T., Kaski, S., Lagus, K., and Kohonen, T. (1997). Websom - self-organizing maps of document collections. In *Proc. of WSOM*.

Huang, E., Cheng, S. H., Dressman, H., Pittman, J., and et al. (2003). Gene expression predictors of breast cancer outcomes. *The Lancet*, 361:1590–1596.

Hubert, A. (1985). Comparing partitions. *J. of Classification*, 2:193–198.

Hubert, L. and Schulz, J. (1976). Quadratic assignment as a general data-analysis strategy. *Br. J. Math. Stat. Psychol.*, 29:190–241.

Hur, A. B., Elisseeff, A., and Guyon, I. (2002). A stability based method for discovering structure in clustered data. In *Pacific Symposium on Biocomputing*, pages 6–17.

Jaccard, P. (1908). Nouvelles recherches sur la distribution florale. *Bul. Soc. Vaudoise Sci. Nat.*, 44:223–270.

Jain, A. K., Murty, M. N., and Flynn, P. J. (1999). Data clustering: a review. *ACM Comput. Surv.*, 31(3):264–323.

Jardine, N. and Sibson, R. (1971). *Mathematical Taxonomy*. John Wiley and Sons.

Johnson, N. L., Kotz, S., and Balakrishnan, N. (1997). *Discrete multivariate distributions*. Wiley.

Karlin, S. and Burge, C. (1995). Dinucleotide relative abundance extremes: a genomic signature. *Trends Genet*, 11(7):283–290.

Kaski, S., Nikkilä, J., and Kohonen, T. (1998). Methods for interpreting a self-organized map in data analysis. In *Proc. of ESANN*.

Kell, D. B. and Oliver, S. G. (2004). Here is the evidence, now what is the hypothesis? the complementary roles of inductive and hypothesis-driven science in the post-genomic era. *BioEssays*, 26:99–105.

Kendall (1938). A new measure of rank correlation. *Biometrika*, 30:81–89.

Kerr, M. and Churchill, G. (2001). Bootstrapping cluster analysis: Assessing the reliability of conclusions from microarray experiments. *PNAS*, Early Edition:1–5.

Kiviluoto, K. (1996). Topology Preservation in Self-Organizing Maps. *ICNN*, pages 294–299.

Kleiner, B. and Hartigan, J. (1981). Representing points in many dimension by trees and castles. *J. Am. Stat. Ass.*, 76:260–9.

Kluger, Y., Basri, R., Chang, J., and Gerstein, M. (2003). Spectral biclustering of microarray data: Coclustering genes and conditions. *Genome Res.*, 13(4):703–16.

Kohonen, T. (1989). *Self-Organization and Associative Memory*. Springer.

Kohonen, T. (1990). The self-organizing map. *Proc. of the IEEE*, 78(9):1464–80.

Kohonen, T. (2001). *Self Organizing Maps*. Springer-Verlag, Berlin.

Kraus, M. and Ertl, T. (2001). Interactive data exploration with customized glyphs. In Skala, V., editor, *WSCG 2001 Conference Proceedings*.

Lamping, J., Rao, R., and Pirolli, P. (1995). A focus + context technique based on hyperbolic geometry for visualizing large hierarchies. In *Human Factors in Computing Systems*. ACM.

BIBLIOGRAPHY

Levine, E. and Domany, E. (2001). Resampling methods for unsupervised estimation of cluster validity. *Neural Comput.*, 13:2573–2593.

Li, W. H. (1997). *Molecular evolution*. Sinauer Associates, Sunderland, MA.

Madeira, S. and Oliviera, A. (2004). Biclustering algorithms for biological data analysis: a survey. *IEEE Trans. Comput. Biol. Bioinformatics*, 1:24–45.

Margulies, M., Egholm, M., Altman, W., Attiya, S., and et al. (2005). Genome sequencing in microfabricated high-density picolitre reactors. *Nature*, 437:376–80.

Martin, C., Diaz, N. N., Ontrup, J., and Nattkemper, T. W. (2007). Genome feature exploration using hyperbolic Self-Organising Maps. *WSOM*.

Maulik, U. and Bandyopadhyay, S. (2002). Performance evaluation of some clustering algorithms and validity indices. *IEEE transactions PAMI*, 24(12):1650–1654.

McHardy, A. C., G, M. H., Tsirigos, A., Hugenholtz, P., and Rigoutsos, I. (2007). Accurate phylogenetic classification of variable-length DNA fragments. *Nature Methods*, 4(1):63–72.

Mewes, H., Frishman, D., Guldener, U., Mannhaupt, G., Mayer, K., Mokrejs, M., Morgenstern, B., Munsterkotter, M., Rudd, S., and Weil, B. (2002). MIPS: a database for genomes and protein sequences. *Nucleic Acid Res.*, 30:31–34.

Nattkemper, T. W. (2005). The SOM reef - a new metaphoric visualization approach for self organizing maps. *WSOM*.

Noh, J.-y. and Neumann, U. (1998). A survey of facial modeling and animation techniques. Technical Report 99-705, USC Technical Report.

Ochs (2003). Microarray in cancer: Research and applications. *Biotechn.*, 34:4–15.

Ontrup, J. (2008). *Semantic Visualization with Hyperbolic Self-Organizing Maps - a novel approach for exploring structure in large data sets*. PhD thesis, Faculty of Technology, Bielefeld University, Germany.

Ontrup, J. and Ritter, H. (2005). Hyperbolic Self-Organizing Maps for Semantic Navigation. In *NIPS*.

Ontrup, J. and Ritter, H. (2006). Large Scale Data Exploration with the Hierarchical Growing Hyberbolic SOM. *Neural Networks, Special Issue on New Developments in Self-Organizing Systems*, 19:751–761.

Overbeek, R., Begley, T., Butler, R. M., Choudhuri, J. V., and et al. (2005). The subsystems approach to genome annotation and its use in the project to annotate 1000 genomes. *Nucleic Acids Res*, 33(17):5691–5702. Evaluation Studies.

Perou, C. M., Sorlie, T., Eisen, M. B., van de Rijn, M., Jeffrey, S. S., Rees, C. A., Pollack, J. R., Ross, D. T., Johnsen, H., Akslen, L. A., Fluge, O., Pergamenschikov, A., Williams, C., Zhu, S. X., LØnning, P. E., BØrresen-Dale, A.-L., Brown, P. O., , and Botstein, D. (2000). Molecular portraits of human breast tumours. *Nature*, 406:747–752.

Pickett, R. M. and Grinstein, G. G. (1988). Iconographics displays for visualizing multidimensional data. In *Proc. IEEE Conf. on Systems, Man, and Cybernetics*, pages 514–9.

Qi, J., Wang, B., and Hao, B.-I. (2004). Whole proteome prokaryote phylogeny without sequence alignment: a K-string composition approach. *J Mol Evol*, 58(1):1–11. Comparative Study.

Quackenbush, J. (2001). Computational analysis of microarray data. *Nat Rev Genet*, 2(6):418–27.

Rahimi, A. and Recht, B. (2004). Clustering with normalized cuts is clustering with a hyperplane. *Statistical Learning in Computer Vision*.

Ramaswamy, S., Tamayo, P., Rifkin, R., Mukherjee, S., Yeang, C., Angelo, M., Ladd, C., Reich, M., Latulippe, E., Mesirov, J., Poggio, T., Gerald, W., Loda, M., Lander, E., and Golub, T. (2001). Multiclass cancer diagnosis using tumor gene expression signatures. *PNAS*, 98(26):15149–15154.

Rand, W. (1971). Objective criteria for the evaluation of clustering methods. *J. of the American Statistical Association*, 66:846–850.

Rauber, A. and Merkl, D. (2001). Automatic labeling of self-organizing maps for information retrieval. *JSRIS*, 10(10):23–45.

Ribarsky, M., Ayers, E., Eble, J., and Mukherjea, S. (1994). Glyphmaker: Creating customized visualizations of complex data. *IEEE Computer*, 27(7):57–64.

Ritter, H. (1999). *Self-organizing maps in non-euclidian spaces*, pages 97–110. Amer Elsevier.

Romesburg, H. (1984). *Cluster Analysis for Researchers*. Belmont California: Lifetime Learning Publications.

Rousseeuw, P. (1987). Silhouettes: a graphical aid to the interpretation and validation of cluster analysis. *J. Comput. Appl. Math.*, 20:53–56.

Sachs, L. (2002). *Angewandte Statistik*. Springer, 10 edition.

Salton, G., Wong, A., and Yang, C. S. (1975). A Vector Space Model for Automatic Indexing. *Information Retrieval*, 18(11):613–620.

Sanger, F., Nicklen, S., and Coulson, A. R. (1977). DNA sequencing with chain-terminating inhibitors. *PNAS*, 74:5463–7.

Shamir, R. and Sharan, R. (2001). Algorithmic approaches to clustering gene expression data. In Jiang, T., Smith, T., Xu, Y., and Zhang, M. Q., editors, *Current Topics in Computational Biology*. MIT press.

Shaw, C. D., Hall, J. A., Blahut, C., Ebert, D. S., and Roberts, D. A. (1999). Using shape to visualize multivariate data. In *Workshop on New Paradigms in Information Visualization and Manipulation*, pages 17–20.

Shi, J. and Malik, J. (2000). Normalized cuts and image segmentation. *IEEE PAMI*, 22(8):888–905.

Siegel, J., Farrell, E., Goldwyn, R., and Friedman, H. (1972). The surgical implication of physiologic patterns in myocardial infarction shock. *Surgery*, 72:126–41.

Smith, M., Taffler, R., and White, L. (2002). Cartoon graphics in the communication of accounting information for management decision making. *Journal of Applied Management Accounting Research*, 1(1):31–50.

Smolkin, M. and Ghosh, D. (2003). Cluster stability scores for microarray data in cancer studies. *BMC Bioinformatics*, 4(36).

Spoerri, A. (1993). Infocrystal: a visual tool for information retrieval & management. In *Proceedings of the second international conference on Information and knowledge management*, Washington, D.C., United States. ACM Press.

Sterky, F. and Lundeberg, J. (2000). Sequence analysis of genes and genomes. *J Biotechnology*, 76:1–31.

Steuer, R. and Selbig, P. H. J. (2006). Validation and functional annotation of expression-based clusters based on gene ontology. *BMC Bioinformatics*, 7(380).

Stuart, G. W., Moffett, K., and Leader, J. J. (2002). A comprehensive vertebrate phylogeny using vector representations of protein sequences from whole genomes. *Mol Biol Evol*, 19(4):554–562.

Tamayo, P., Slonim, D., and et al. (1999). Interpreting patterns of gene expression with self-organizing maps: methods and application to hematopoietic differentiation. *PNAS*, 96:2907–12.

Tavazoie, S., Hughes, J. D., Campbell, M. J., Cho, R. J., and Church, G. M. (1999). Systematic determination of genetic network architecture. *Nat. Gen.*, 22:281–5.

Teeling, H., Waldmann, J., Lombardot, T., Bauer, M., and Glockner, F. (2004). TETRA: a web-service and a stand-alone program for the analysis and comparison of tetranucleotide usage patterns in DNA sequences. *BMC Bioinf*, 5(1):163.

BIBLIOGRAPHY

Thalamuthu, A., Mukhopadhyay, I., Zheng, X., and G.C.Tseng (2006). Evaluation and comparison of gene clustering methods in microarray analysis. *Bioinformatics*, 22(19):2405–2412.

Tjaden, B. (2006). An approach for clustering gene expression data with error information. *BMC Bioinformatics*, 7(17).

Toronen, P. (2004a). *Analysis of gene expression data using clustering and functional classifications*. PhD thesis, A. I. Virtanen Institute for Molecular Sciences, Neulaniementie 2, P.O. Box 1627, FIN-70211 Kuopio, Finland.

Toronen, P. (2004b). Selection of informative clusters from hierarchical cluster tree with gene classes. *BMC Bioinformatics*, 5(1)(32).

Ultsch, A. (1993a). Self organizing neural networks for visualization and classification. In et al., O., editor, *Information and Classification*, pages 307–13. Springer.

Ultsch, A. (1993b). Self organizing neural networks for visualization and classification. In et al., O., editor, *Information and Classification*, pages 307–13. Springer.

van de Vijver, M. J., Yudong, D., van't Veer, L., and et al., D. H. (2002). A gene-expression signature as a predictor of survival in breast cancer. *The New Eng J Med*, 347(25):1999–2009.

van't Veer, L. J., Dai, H., van de Vijver, M. J., Y D He, A. A. M. H., Mao, M., Peterse, H. L., van der Kooy, K., Marton, M. J., and et al., A. T. W. (2002). Gene expression profiling predicts clinical outcome of breast cancer. *Nature*, 415:530–6.

Venna, J. and Kaski, S. (2005). Local multidimensional scaling with controlled tradeoff between trustworthiness and continuity. *Proc. WSOM*, pages 695–703.

Venter, J. and et al. (304). Environmental genome shotgun sequencing of the sargasso sea. *Science*, 66-74:2004.

Vesanto, J. (1999). Som-based visualization methods. *Intell. Data Anal.*, 3:111–26.

Vesanto, J. and Alhoneimi, E. (2000). Clustering of the self-organizing map. *IEEE Transactions on Neural Networks*, 11:586–600.

Wang, F., Wang, J., and Zhang, C. (2005). Spectral feature analysis. *IJCNN*.

Wang, J. and et al. (2002). Clustering of the SOM easily reveals distinct gene expression patterns: results of a reanalysis of lymphoma study. *BMC Bioinf.*, 3(36).

Weiss, Y. (1999). Segmentation using eigenvectors: a unifying view. *Proc. IEEE Intl. Conf. on Computer Vision*, 2:975–82.

Wheeler, D. L., Church, D. M., Lash, A. E., Leipe, D. D., and et al. (2002). Database resources of the National Center for Biotechnology Information: 2002 update. *Nucleic Acids Res*, 30(1):13–16.

Wu, S. and Chow, T. W. S. (2004). Clustering of the self-organizing map using a clustering validity index based on inter-cluster and intra-cluster density. *Pattern Recognition*, 37:175–188.

Wu, Z. and Leahy, R. (1993). An optimal graph theoretic approach to data clustering: theory and its application to image segmentation. *IEEE PAMI*, 15(11):1101–13.

Xing, E. and Karp, R. (2001). CLIFF: Clustering of high–dimensional microarray data via iterative feature filtering using normalized cuts. *Bioinformatics*, 17(Suppl. 1):306–15.

Yang, C. C., Chen, H., and Hong, K. K. (1999). Visualization tools for self-organizing maps. In *Proc. of the 4th ACM conf. on Digital libraries*, pages 258–9.

Yang, Y. H., Dudoit, S., Luu, P., Lin, D. M., Peng, V., Ngai, J., and Speed, T. P. (2002). Normalization for cDNA microarray data: a robust composite method addressing single and multiple slide systematic variation. *Nucleic Acids Research*, 30(4):e15, 1–10.

Yeung, K., Haynor, D., and Ruzzo, W. (2001). Validating clustering for gene expression data. *Bioinformatics*, 17(4):309–318.

Yeung, K. Y. and et al. (2001). Model-based clustering and data transformation for gene expression data. *Bioinformatics*, 17:977–987.

Yu, S. X. and Shi, J. (2003). Multiclass spectral clustering. In *ICCV03*, pages 313–9, Nice, France.

Zelnik-Manor, L. and Perona, P. (2005). Self-tuning spectral clustering. In Saul, L. K., Weiss, Y., and Bottou, L., editors, *Advances in Neural Information Processing Systems 17*, pages 1601–8. MIT Press, Cambridge, MA.

Zuckerkandl, E. and Pauling, L. (1965). Molecules as documents of evolutionary history. *J Theor Biol*, 8(2):357–366.

Die VDM Verlagsservicegesellschaft sucht für wissenschaftliche Verlage abgeschlossene und herausragende

Dissertationen, Habilitationen, Diplomarbeiten, Master Theses, Magisterarbeiten usw.

für die kostenlose Publikation als Fachbuch.

Sie verfügen über eine Arbeit, die hohen inhaltlichen und formalen Ansprüchen genügt, und haben Interesse an einer honorarvergüteten Publikation?

Dann senden Sie bitte erste Informationen über sich und Ihre Arbeit per Email an *info@vdm-vsg.de*.

Sie erhalten kurzfristig unser Feedback!

VDM Verlagsservicegesellschaft mbH
Dudweiler Landstr. 99
D - 66123 Saarbrücken

Telefon +49 681 3720 174
Fax +49 681 3720 1749

www.vdm-vsg.de

Die VDM Verlagsservicegesellschaft mbH vertritt

Printed by Books on Demand GmbH, Norderstedt / Germany